THE DEFINITIVE GUIDE TO

THE HOTCHKIN COURSE - WOODHALL SPA

Richard A Latham

1st Edition December 2004

Published in two versions - standard and special edition.

The special edition is limited to 100 copies only.

ISBN 0-9549172-0-0

Published by Radial Sports Publishing Limited

Kaim End, Hudnall Common, Little Gaddesden, Hertfordshire HP4 1QJ

www.radialsportspublishing.com

Designed, printed and bound in the United Kingdom

DEDICATIONS

To Sylvia, my wife, for her unerring support and encouragement.

To my children Christopher and Suzy.

To Neil Hotchkin who spent many hours checking the facts and offering advice - always with complete verve and modesty.

ACKNOWLEDGEMENTS

We would like to thank the many organisations and individuals for their assistance during this project:

Eric Hepworth for the many hours he spent taking the wonderful collection of photographs included in this book
● David Duckering of Strokesaver for providing hole graphics and aerial photographs ● Colin Reiners and Lys-ann Bale for their patience in reviewing the text
● Roger Labbett for his support in providing information for the section on flora and fauna ● David Robinson for his assistance in defining local geology
● The Horncastle News for allowing us to reproduce quotes from several editions
● The publishers of Golf Weekly for allowing us to reproduce photographs and passages of text from old editions of Golf Illustrated and Golfing.
In particular, Linda Manigan who was extremely helpful in supplying information and, the Editor, Peter Masters for his encouragement and enthusiasm
● Golf Monthly ● Golf Magazine of America ● Lincolnshire Echo ● Lincolnshire Archives ● Lincoln Library ● The Cottage Museum in Woodhall Spa
● British Newspaper Library ● The Lincolnshire Naturalist's Union, particularly Paul Kirby, Vi Wilkin, Zella Harris and Irene Weston
● Lincolnshire Life ● Country Life ● R&A ● USGA ● The English Golf Union for permission to use photographs
● Woodhall Spa Golf Club for use of their invaluable albums ● Wave Creative Communications for their design input ● Wayzgoose Print for their input on printing and publishing
● Many individuals including Douglas Adams, Rob Chappelhow, Iain Cumming, Ben Fawcett, John Flanders, Sallie Hotchkin,
Paul Fletcher, Bob Grant, David Hamilton, Alan Jackson, David Longmore, Rhod McEwan, John Moreton, Richard Palmer,
Ralph Pickering, John Skeet, Donald Steel, Stuart Whaley, Struan Wiley and Peter Wisbey.

There were many contributors and we sincerely apologise if there were any omissions.

There were also a large number of publications that were used during the research phase.
Where a quote has been specifically used due credit has been given in relevant chapters. Once again, we apologise for any omissions.

CONTENTS

Sir Michael Bonallack receiving the English Amateur Championship Trophy at Woodhall Spa in 1967

I have long been of the opinion that some of the finest golf courses in the world are to be found at clubs that are effectively controlled by a 'benevolent dictator'. This includes such famous clubs as Augusta, Cypress Point, Pine Valley and Woodhall Spa.

It is no coincidence that these courses have been able to survive the fate suffered by many others, which have seen countless changes made to their layouts by well intentioned but misguided green committees, or sometimes even by the Captain for the year, and which usually totally ignore the original thinking of the architect.

Whilst it is true that the four I have singled out have seen some changes, these have been made with a view to preserving the architect's strategy, but making allowances for the increased distances the golf ball can now be hit.

Colonel Hotchkin's views on architecture are perfectly exemplified in the re-design of his course at Woodhall Spa and his son Neil ensured that these qualities were fiercely protected and thereby still hold as good today as they did seventy years ago.

Golf was originally a natural game, in the sense that the architect blended the course into existing surroundings, making use of any natural features and contours that happened to be on the site, but not concentrating on making one really spectacular hole to the possible detriment of a number of others. How I hate the modern term "signature hole". The great architects designed eighteen holes equally memorable, albeit for different reasons.

I first played the course at Woodhall Spa almost fifty years ago and can honestly say that I fell in love with it from first sight, even if I found it a little too demanding for the skills I had at that time.

Every hole is unique to itself, and each of them has features which make it different to the other seventeen, with the combination of heather, sand, trees and deep cavernous bunkers providing as good a test of every aspect of the game as you are ever likely to find.

Not only do you have to drive the ball well, but you also have to be able to play the high pitch shot as well as the pitch and run. There is also a nice balance, which favours neither those who fade the ball, nor those who draw it. The par three holes are of varying lengths, with the two shortest probably providing the greatest potential for disaster, as do some of the shorter par fours.

To play golf on The Hotchkin course is one of the most pleasurable and testing experiences the game has to offer. I am delighted that Richard Latham has worked so hard to create 'The Definitive Guide to The Hotchkin Course' and feel honoured that he has asked me to write the foreword.

Woodhall Spa and Neil and Sallie Hotchkin will always have a very special place in my golfing memories, both for the happy times I spent in their company and on this magnificent golf course.

Sir Michael F Bonallack OBE

November 2004

TOP 100 COURSES IN THE WORLD

1	Pine Valley	US
2	Cypress Point	US
3	Muirfield	Scotland
4	Shinnecock Hills	US
5	Augusta National	US
6	St Andrews (Old Course)	Scotland
7	Pebble Beach	US
8	Royal Melbourne (Composite)	Australia
9	Pinehurst (No 2)	US
10	Royal County Down	Northern Ireland
11	Sand Hills	US
12	Royal Portrush (Dunluce)	Northern Ireland
13	Ballybunion (Old)	Ireland
14	Merion (East)	US
15	Oakmont	US
16	Royal Dornoch	Scotland
17	Turnberry (Ailsa)	Scotland
18	Winged Foot (West)	US
19	Pacific Dunes	US
20	National Golf Links of America	US
21	Kingston Heath	Australia
22	Seminole	US
23	Prairie Dunes	US
24	Crystal Downs	US
25	Oakland Hills (South)	US
26	Carnoustie (Championship)	Scotland
27	San Francisco	US
28	Royal Birkdale	England
29	Fishers Island	US
30	Bethpage (Black)	US
31	Chicago	US
32	Royal St George's	England
33	The Country Club (Championship)	US
34	Casa de Campo	Dominican Republic
35	Hirono	Japan
36	Riviera	US
37	Muirfield Village	US
38	Royal Troon (Old)	Scotland
39	Olympic (Lake)	US
40	Portmarnock	Ireland
41	Southern Hills	US
42	Oak Hill (East)	US
43	New South Wales	Australia
44	Sunningdale (Old)	England
45	Baltusrol (Lower)	US
46	Woodhall Spa	England
47	Morfontaine	France
48	The Golf Club	US
49	Kauri Cliffs	New Zealand
50	Royal Adelaide	Australia
51	Shoreacres	US
52	Medinah (No 3)	US
53	Whistling Straits (Straits)	US
54	Royal Lytham & St Annes	England
55	Garden City	US
56	Loch Lomond	Scotland
57	TPC Sawgrass (Stadium)	US
58	Inverness	US
59	Los Angeles (North)	US
60	Maidstone	US
61	Quaker Ridge	US
62	Ganton	England
63	Camargo	US
64	Highland Links	Canada
65	Kingsbarns	Scotland
66	Winged Foot (East)	US
67	Harbour Town	US
68	Cabo del Sól (Ocean)	Mexico
69	Somerset Hills	US
70	Durban	S Africa
71	Scioto	US
72	Royal Liverpool	England
73	Lahinch	Ireland
74	Bandon Dunes	US
75	Naruo	Japan
76	Cruden Bay	Scotland
77	Valderrama	Spain
78	Wentworth (West)	England
79	Kiawah Island (Ocean)	US
80	Kawana	Japan
81	Spyglass Hill	US
82	Walton Heath (Old)	England
83	World Woods (Pine Barrens)	US
84	Ocean Forest	US
85	Valley Cub of Montecito	US
86	Congressional (Blue)	US
87	Peachtree	US
88	Wade Hampton	US
89	Shadow Creek	US
90	Cherry Hills	US
91	Baltimore (Five Farms East)	US
92	Yeamans Hall	US
93	El Saler	Spain
94	Homestead (Cascades)	US
95	St George's	Canada
96	The Honors Course	US
97	East Lake	US
98	European Club	Ireland
99	Paraparaumu Beach	New Zealand
100	Colonial	US

Reproduced with the kind permission of *Golf Magazine of America*

'It is, I think, the best course, using best in the most comprehensive sense, that I have played on in Britain...'
- *Henry Longhurst (1935).*

How did a course in a quiet village in the middle of secluded Lincolnshire, away from the spotlight of major professional championships and television coverage, become one of the greatest courses in the world? This is the story of how The Hotchkin course at Woodhall Spa was created. Ranked continuously in the world's top 100 courses since such ratings have been kept, the unique qualities of The Hotchkin course may be attributed to the dedication of Colonel S V Hotchkin, who, in his constant search for perfection, created something unique.

Writing in **Country Life** in 1927, Bernard Darwin described the essence of what made Woodhall Spa *the best and most charming course I have ever seen.'*

'Dealing, then, only in generalities, I will say that there are the usual ingredients from which the best inland golf is made, heather and sand. The sand is particularly fine and there is an unlimited quantity of it, with the result that the bunkers are on a seaside and magnificent scale. What impressed me most of all was that this course, which looks so beautifully natural, is, in a sense, completely artificial. All those fine big bunkers which look as if they had "just growed", were dug by the hand of man, and every blade of grass has had to be sowed. ... Finally, there is the charm of restfulness and tranquillity which belongs to certain courses that I love much... it possesses a delicious, countrified feeling, which it could not lose no matter how many golfers were on it.'

During the early years, the Hotchkin family provided land and significant financial backing for the project, particularly during the major redevelopment phases running up to the First World War. The Colonel had been involved in every aspect of the Club since the days of the old nine hole course and had worked very closely with both Vardon and Colt. In the 1920s he redesigned the bunkering and most of the green sites, constantly striving to produce the best inland course in Britain. After his death in 1953 the Colonel's son, Neil, who stoutly defended his father's architectural principles, ensured that the course's distinctive challenge continues today as it did for golfers a hundred years ago. With the primary objective of protecting the future of both the course and the Club, Neil Hotchkin sold the course and facilities to the English Golf Union in 1995. When the former Ryder Cup Captain, Bernard Gallagher, visited Woodhall Spa in 2002 he stated that *"the Hotchkin course was one of the best on the planet"* - a fitting tribute to all those who have been involved over the past 100 years.

This account will also provide an insight into golf course architecture, illustrating how the course has changed in response to developments in equipment, while at the same time, retaining its unique sporting identity.

THE HOTCHKIN COURSE – WOODHALL SPA

CHAPTER 1 ~ THE BEGINNING OF GOLF IN WOODHALL SPA

Golf was first introduced to Woodhall Spa in 1890 when a nine hole course was laid out. By 1895, a second site had to be found when land was required for village expansion. Only eight years later and for the same reason as before, it became clear that yet another site would have to be found. The Hotchkin family kindly offered a piece of their land as an alternative venue, which would provide the Golf Club with a permanent home. In 1903, work commenced and the foundation stone of what was to become a truly great championship course was laid.

Early golf in Woodhall Spa

The three locations in Woodhall Spa where golf has been played are indicated on the map. Today there is no physical evidence of the first two locations as buildings and gardens now occupy these sites. The first two locations are discussed in this chapter, with the final location being the main subject of the book.

Location One

The first site was on land bounded by the old railway line, Abbey Lane and Tattershall Road. The *Horncastle News and South Lindsey Advertiser** reported on the introduction of golf to Woodhall Spa. One such passage (published on 12th July 1890) stated that *'the links have been laid out at Mr. Copping's large field on the Tattershall Road.'* The key words in this statement are 'laid out' as opposed to 'built'. Prior to 1900 most courses were laid out taking the natural features of the land into consideration. Earth moving was minimal, as the only method would have been manual labour and horses at this time. The use of mechanical equipment to

shape fairways and greens in different land forms was generally not available until the late 1930s.

Many inland golf courses built in Victorian times consisted of square tees and greens and simple unnatural looking hazards were placed in front of the teeing ground to catch poorly struck tee shots.

No evidence of the course layout could be found and it is assumed that the holes were of basic design. Woodhall Spa Golf Club itself was formed in 1891 and the Secretary was reported as being E V Stokoe. By 1895, the village was expanding and the land occupied by the golf course was required for building houses. From newspaper reports, it would appear that the Club had little time to find another site.

Location Two

About sixty acres of flat land was made available on both sides of the Stixwold Road and another nine hole course was laid out. One interesting and significant fact from the early newspaper reports is that the course was laid out and ready for play in three months!

The first three holes together with the ninth were played on one side of the road on land that is now the Petwood Hotel gardens and the Kinema in the Woods. Holes four to eight were played on the other side, an area that is now part of Jubilee Park. The diagram on page 10 illustrates the layout of the course and the yardages of each hole. The total length of the course was 2,327 yards and the course consisted of eight par 4's and a par 3.

True to the principles of architecture of the era, it is interesting to note from the course layout diagram just how many tee shots required a carry over hazards placed directly in front of the tee.

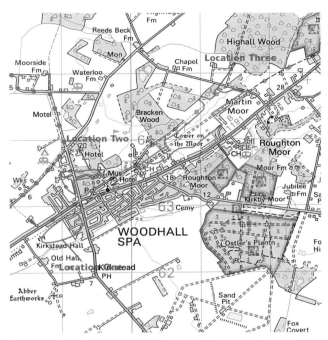

Reproduced from Ordnance Survey mapping on behalf of Her Majesty's Stationery Office © Crown Copyright 100043472

* A weekly newspaper still being published today and now called the *Horncastle News*

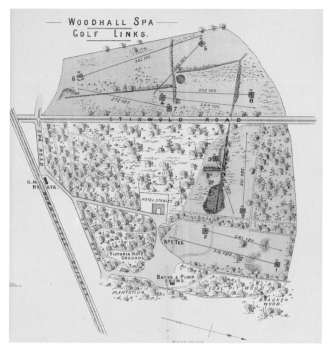

Course layout - Location Two

Dr. Michael J Hurdzan explains this philosophy in his book called *Golf Course Architecture* - 'In general, most golf courses at that time were laid out by golf professionals of accomplished playing ability. These men felt that the greatest evil in golf was the topped shot. Until the beginning of the twentieth century, golf balls were difficult to get airborne. The old 'feathery' golf ball was notoriously difficult for players to hit in the air. But the feathery ball would run along the hard ground nearly as far as a shot properly played through the air. To penalize such inelegantly struck shots, the early architects built steep sided, unnatural looking elevated earthworks placed directly across the line of play.'

It would seem that this design style (known as 'penal', where the only way to reach a target is to carry a specific hazard) was the preferred choice and existed until the early 1900s, even with the introduction of the gutta-percha ball of the 1850s. The 'gutty' ball flew further than the 'feathery' but those laying out courses maintained the same penal philosophy and simply adjusted the hazard placements.

The length of a solid drive with a hickory shafted driver and a 'gutty' ball would be in the region of 190 yards. However, the introduction of the rubber cored ball in 1902 had a dramatic effect on the game and a well struck drive would typically travel 220 yards.

The Club flourished over the next eight years and many competitions and events were reported in local newspapers and national golf publications. In the 1898 *Golfer's Annual,* a reference was made to the Woodhall Spa Golf and Tennis Club: 'Instituted 1891. A nine hole course, the first holes of which are very prettily situated in the grounds of the Spa and the Victoria Hotel, and within three minutes walk of the Woodhall Spa station, on the GNR. The greens are good, length of course about a mile and three quarters. New clubhouse for teas, drinks etc. (members only). No conveyance from station unless ordered. Capt. E V Stokoe; Hon. Sec and Treas C J Williams; Asst. Sec J Hucknall; Greenkeeper Frederick Norris. Membership 50.' One point to note is the reference to the name which includes 'Tennis Club'. Tennis courts were available for play but it is unusual to have included this facility in the name of the club*.

In the 1900-1 *Golfing Annual,* another reference is made to Woodhall Spa Golf and Tennis Club. Annual subscriptions were £1 or £2 for a family and the membership had increased to 60. Charges for visitors were two shillings and sixpence per week or five shillings for a family. A reference to a par of 35 was also made in this account.

The Lincolnshire Amateur Championship was played over the course in May 1902. However, it is likely that the biggest moment for the Club in terms of playing was an exhibition match played in 1903. Harry Vardon had been employed to look at a site for a new 18 hole course and during his stay, he played an exhibition match. A rare set of photographs commemorating this event on 24th January 1903 are included. Vardon played against the best ball of two officers of the Club, A Wallace and T P Stokoe. Over 200 locals

* During the research of this project references were also found to Woodhall Spa and District Golf Club in the publication *Golfing*. In a list of 'extinct golf clubs' reference was made to this name stating that the club no longer existed after 1896. However, it is not clear whether this was a different club playing over the same course as Woodhall Spa Golf Club (like some Scottish clubs) or whether the Club simply changed its name. The author assumes it was the latter case as it would have been highly unlikely that there were enough resident golfers in the area to fill two clubs, coupled with the lack of transport in those days.

turned up to watch the match and Vardon thrilled the onlookers with a dazzling display, beating the old course record in each of the three nine hole rounds as well as his opponents.

Vardon's scores were:

1st Round   3, 5, 3, 3, 4, 4, 5, 5, 3 = 35
2nd Round   5, 4, 5, 3, 3, 4, 3, 5, 4 = 36
3rd Round   4, 4, 3, 2, 6, 4, 4, 5, 4 = 36

The *Horncastle News* reported the match: *'The start was a sensational one, Vardon taking the first hole in a perfect 3. Except for a short putt missed on the second green, and the fact that he found the bunker with his brassie at the 7th hole, the rest of his round was perfect golf, which could hardly have been improved upon. At the ninth hole his drive was phenomenal, the ball lying level with the flag, a distance of 260 yards. It was a great drive, as the ball gets no assistance from the lie of the ground, and has to be absolutely straight to avoid the two bunkers which guard the green. In both his subsequent rounds he carried the bunker at the seventh hole with his second shot reaching the green, and holed out on one occasion in 3. He finished 11 up on the 27 holes against his opponents, being at the same time 10 up against the bogey score.'*

Vardon driving from the 3rd tee

Stokoe putting on the 4th green

Wallace putting on the 3rd green

Vardon putting on the 4th green

THE HOTCHKIN COURSE – WOODHALL SPA

CHAPTER 2 ~ BIRTH OF A CHAMPIONSHIP COURSE

By the turn of the century, golf had become an added attraction to the many visitors who were frequenting the spa to enjoy the healing properties of the water. They came from London by train for both short and long breaks, mostly staying at the Victoria and Royal Hotels. One paper reported that over 47,000 people visited Woodhall Spa in 1889. Some of the visitors played golf and the operators of the railway, the Great Northern Railway Company, actively encouraged golfers by selling tickets that included rounds of golf. One publication in 1910 detailed weekend golf breaks, staying at the Victoria Hotel for £2 15s which included full board, golf and a first class rail return from King's Cross*.

This era also coincided with a significant increase in the popularity of golf and many new courses were being built. This fact is best illustrated by noting that in 1886, there were reported to be 171 courses in the UK. By 1914, there were over 2,500 clubs listed in *Nisbet's* Directory of Golf Clubs. Significant improvements in golf equipment at this time were also making the game more enjoyable.

Vardon's Influence

When the Golf Club faced the challenge of finding a new site in 1903, the Hotchkin family offered a sandy tract of land off the Horncastle Road. This land was essentially moorland and was mainly used for hunting. Stafford Vere Hotchkin was a prominent member of the Golf Club, playing off a single figure handicap, and a local landowner. The offer of this venue was very attractive as the owner was guaranteeing a permanent home for the Golf Club in the foreseeable future and the rent was extremely reasonable (£50 per annum). The Golf Club gratefully accepted his offer.

There were now two important decisions to make: 1) how the course should be funded and, 2) who should be employed to advise on an appropriate layout. Financial support was offered by the Hotchkin family and smaller donations from other sources were also promised. With regard to laying out the course, the leading players were considered to be the experts on all matters pertaining to golf including course design, construction and maintenance. One of the most successful professionals at that time was Harry Vardon, a prolific golfer who by 1903 had won four Open Championships and the US Open. He was the Professional at Ganton at that time but was about to move to South Herts in London where he would remain until he retired. He was duly asked to complete an initial assessment of the site and visited Woodhall Spa for the first time at the beginning of 1903.

Vardon considered the site to be most appropriate and commented that it was similar in character to courses in Surrey. In terms of course design experience, Woodhall Spa would certainly have been one of Vardon's early 18 hole courses (in fact, one study has suggested that Woodhall Spa was only Vardon's fourth 18 hole design).

Work started on transforming the site shortly afterwards and the immediate challenge was to overcome the lack of fertile soil and grass cover. *Golf Illustrated* reported that *'to form the greens tons of hard cemented sand had to be excavated.'* It was reported that there were several set-backs during construction, mainly due to a wet summer in 1903 which resulted in the grass seed being washed away, followed by drought conditions in 1904. Large quantities of seed were purchased from Crowders, a local firm in Horncastle. Two years on from the start of the project, on Saturday 25th February 1905, holes were cut on the greens for the first time. It is not

* The importance of rail travel to the development of golf in general is eloquently presented in a book called *'Golf and the Railway Connection'* written by Ian Nalder. However, in this case it is important to note that the railway line was built because of the popularity of the spa, not the golf course.

clear how many visits Harry Vardon made to the site during the construction phase, if indeed at all. However, there is no doubt from various reports that the main responsibility for construction was shouldered by Hotchkin and T P Stokoe.

The course was constructed by manual labour with assistance from horses, carts and scoops. As mechanical equipment was not available in those days, horse drawn cultivators and spike harrows would also have been used.

The construction of this course would have been a major exercise, as virtually the whole site was covered with sand and gravel, which was extremely hard and compacted in places. It is likely that the reason for so many large bunkers was that there was an abundance of natural sand and it saved large areas from being seeded. The *Horncastle News* (25th March 1905) reported on the Golf Club's AGM and quoted that *'over 50,000 loads of soil had been carted on to the site.'*

The course had taken just over two years to construct which was considerably longer than the three months taken to lay out the previous nine hole course. Even though the weather conditions had not helped, the difference in time scale shows just how much course design and construction had improved. The result was a layout that tested a range of golfing skills offering a variety of holes.

Without detailed drawings of each hole, it is not possible to be certain about the Vardon design. However, he definitely would not have produced a long course (in 1903, there were not many courses longer than 6,000 yards). Also, the membership would have been used to playing a nine hole course where the longest hole was 382 yards and even though the rubber ball had just been introduced, the distance of the gutty ball would probably have been uppermost in

Horse and scoop

Vardon's mind. A view on the course layout is given on page 21.

An overview of Vardon's life, including his thoughts on golf course architecture is provided in Appendix One. A short summary is provided below:

- Short holes should always be reached with an iron

- Having a short two shot hole that may be reached with a long accurate drive is an interesting option

- Bunkers and other hazards should be placed to test the scratch golfer (not the high handicap golfer). He was not in favour of cross bunkering but where they have to be placed they should be about 130 - 145 yards from the tee (Vardon changed this view in later articles). He preferred to see bunkers placed on either side of the fairway to catch wayward shots. Hazards should be the last features to be placed on a new layout and the course should be played in a variety of conditions before their final positions are decided.

There is no doubt that Vardon applied many of these principles to Woodhall Spa. In particular, the placement of hazards was certainly completed after the course was played.

It was intended that a match be played between Harry Vardon and J H Taylor to test the course but this proved impossible to arrange. A match was therefore played with J H Taylor playing the best ball of three members A H James, W P Costobardie and T P Stokoe. Watched by a large crowd, Taylor went round in 72 beating the members two up. Afterwards he played an exhibition match on the old nine hole course against the Club Professional, Arthur Fosbury, beating him by two holes.

Taylor recommended a number of additional bunker placements and other small changes to the Vardon design. In the March 14th edition of the *Horncastle News*, Taylor is reported as saying: *'There has undoubtedly been a very intelligent interest shown in the construction, the natural features of the ground which lends itself to the game, being utilised to the full with the result that the promoters have succeeded in making a links that take high rank with any inland course in the country, and I venture to predict that this opinion will be endorsed by the great majority of golfers who may have the pleasure of playing it.'* It was also reported that the course would not be open for play until May. *Golf Illustrated* reported that *'the chief feature of the course will be its variety, for, though it will offer plenty of opportunities to the long driver, it has not been laid out like so many modern courses, on a mathematical basis and with sole regard to his requirements. The consideration that is due to the moderate driver has not been forgotten. Monotony has been avoided, and the course should, and almost certainly will, suit players of every kind and description.'*

T P Stokoe

Several local and national publications (*Horncastle News, Woodhall Spa Times and Visitor Lists, Golfing, Golf Illustrated* and others) reported the opening of the course on 24th April 1905. Stokoe had supervised the construction and had also been entrusted with ensuring the financial control of the project. The building of the course had been financed with club funds and a substantial loan of £1,000 from the Hotchkin family. The course had cost £1,305 17s 6d to construct. Interestingly, the 15th Annual General Meeting of Woodhall Spa Golf Club was reported in *Golf Illustrated* in the March 31st edition. The meeting was presided over by Sir Henry Hawley. The balance sheet at February 28th 1905 of the old nine hole course was laid before the meeting and showed that the total assets of the club amounted to £317 1s 9d and liabilities £118 0s 9d, the excess of assets over liabilities being £199 1s.

The officers for the year were elected: President Lord Willoughby de Eresby MP, Vice Presidents T Cheney Garfit and S V Hotchkin; Captain, Honorary Secretary and Treasurer T P Stokoe and Honorary Auditor A Trotter. Hotchkin, Trotter and Stokoe were unanimously elected life members in recognition of their services.

The subject of the clubhouse was also discussed at the AGM. The planned site for it was the field adjoining the first tee and had been planted and laid out as an ornamental pleasure garden. There were also extensive tea lawns, four lawn tennis courts and three full size croquet lawns. Water had also been supplied to the site and the total expenditure was £278 2s 6d. It was decided at this AGM to move the existing clubhouse from the current nine hole venue to the new site. It was reported that a local tradesman named Miller had offered to do this work for a sum not exceeding £10. Further alterations would be necessary and it was decided that the sum of £50 should be found immediately so that work could commence. Stokoe suggested that the money be raised by issuing ten £5 debentures at 5% interest. The shares were immediately taken by those attending the meeting including three purchased by the Hotchkin family.

The Course Opens for Play

At 10.30am on Easter Monday 24th April 1905, a large group assembled on the first tee for the formal opening of the new course. Stokoe conducted the ceremony, stating that he trusted that the new links would prove to be an additional attraction to Woodhall Spa and a source of pleasure to members. After various toasts he asked Mr Stafford Vere Hotchkin to drive the first ball. The course was then officially declared open for play and champagne was drunk from the four main challenge cups (the Hotchkin Bowl, the Benwell Cup, the

Williams Cup and the Stanhope Vase which, incidentally, are still played for today). A competition for the members was organised and the Hotchkin family presented a prize. A match was played between the Woodhall Spa professional, A Fosbury and the club professional at Lincoln, A Earl. Earl won by four and three.

On Friday June 30th 1905, the official opening of the course took place with Lord Willoughby de Eresby MP, the President of the Golf Club, in charge of the proceedings. It had been announced that the links would be officially declared open at 10.30am, but owing to strong winds, the speech making was deferred until after lunch in the large marquee, which had been erected close to the clubhouse. A foursome match was played in the morning and Lord Willoughby and James Braid (the Open Champion) played against Hotchkin and J H Taylor. Another match followed between W P Costobadie and Harry Vardon against J V Wintringham (playing off scratch) and Jack White.

At lunch, Lord Willoughby presided over a large gathering and toasted the future of the Club. The thanks of the Club were given to Hotchkin and Stokoe for their great interest taken during the construction of the course. A professional tournament was held in the afternoon and the winning score was Harry Vardon on 69 (his score beat the old course record of 71 set by Fosbury). Taylor and Braid tied for second place on 73.

The official opening was concluded on Saturday morning, when Taylor, Braid, Vardon and White played in a 36 hole strokeplay exhibition match. Taylor and Braid tied on 140 and they divided first and second prizes. Taylor scored 68 and 72 and Braid the same but in reverse order. Taylor had now broken Vardon's course record set only the day before.

Lord Willoughby de Eresby MP, drives the first ball

Vardon on the 3rd green

Guests at the opening ceremony

White on the 6th tee

J H Taylor on the 16th tee

Braid on the 16th green

Braid approaching the 17th hole

The Course Layout

After an extensive search, a map of the original Vardon layout could not be found. However, a rough idea of the routing has been obtained from a variety of sources including old photographs and media reports. In particular, the following conclusions have been made:

1) Studying the individual gross scores from the competitions held on the 30th June and 1st July, it would appear that the back nine was harder than the front nine. This of course, could have been due to the wind direction on the day but studying scores from future events the same pattern emerges. It would also appear from the newspaper reports that the longer holes were on the back nine.

The actual scores recorded on 30th June 1905 are shown in the table opposite. These scores imply that the 2nd, 6th, 8th, 11th and 16th holes were par 3's; the 1st, 9th and 17th were short par 4's and the long holes were the 7th, 10th, 13th and 18th. Details of the lowest scores from the exhibition match on Saturday 1st July further confirm these thoughts.

2) The April 14th and July 7th 1905 editions of *Golf Illustrated* provided an excellent account of the opening of the course, stating that the holes measured from 102 to 535 yards. The photographs overleaf clearly demonstrate that the layout of the first seven holes was similar to the routing of today.

Hole	1	2	3	4	5	6	7	8	9	Out	10	11	12	13	14	15	16	17	18	In	Score
Harry Vardon	3	3	5	5	4	3	5	3	3	(34)	5	3	4	4	3	4	4	3	5	(35)	69
J H Taylor	3	4	4	5	4	3	6	3	3	(35)	7	3	5	4	4	4	3	3	5	(38)	73
James Braid	4	2	5	4	6	3	5	3	4	(36)	6	2	4	5	4	5	3	3	5	(37)	73
Tom Williamson	4	2	5	5	5	4	5	4	3	(37)	6	3	4	5	5	4	3	3	5	(38)	75
Arthur Fosbury	5	3	4	6	4	3	5	5	4	(37)	8	4	5	5	5	3	3	3	6	(42)	79
Jack White	4	4	7	5	5	3	6	4	4	(42)	5	4	5	6	5	3	4	5	5	(42)	84
Archie Earl	4	3	5	5	4	5	6	4	4	(40)	6	3	5	6	6	4	5	4	5	(44)	84

30th June

Hole	1	2	3	4	5	6	7	8	9	Out	10	11	12	13	14	15	16	17	18	In	Score
J H Taylor	4	3	4	4	4	3	5	3	3	(33)	4	4	4	5	4	4	3	3	4	(35)	68
James Braid	5	3	4	4	3	3	3	3	3	(31)	5	2	5	5	4	3	3	4	6	(37)	68

1st July

left: This photo shows players driving from the 1st tee using a wooden club. The tee marker indicates a distance of 266 yards.

below left: The huge bunker in front of the fourth tee (now the 3rd hole) with the tower in the background.

below: The fourth green is shown here. This hole is now the 3rd green and the green was moved at a later stage by Colonel Hotchkin onto the plateau in the background.

right: The bunker in front of the tee at the 5th hole (now the 4th) is shown here. Note the huge expanse of sand. A small bunker exists today but the outline of the original bunker can still be seen.

bottom right: This bunker was in front of the 6th green (now the 5th hole). The remains can still be seen today.

2nd right: Driving from the 7th tee (now the 6th hole). The tee shown here is the current ladies tee and the pine tree on the left still exists.

Bunkered at the 5th

left and bottom left: These two photos show the ninth hole. It is not clear where this hole was located originally.

Finally, the photograph **(below)** shows golfers driving from the 13th tee. Once again, the location of this hole is not clear but it is thought that it may be the current par 5 14th hole.

These photographs are the only ones of the course that have been traced from this time period.

3) In summary, the **Table 2.1** provides an indication of the type of holes including a par figure (not used in those days) and approximate lengths in 1905.

It is estimated that the total length of the course measured 5,449 yards. Various assumptions have been made in an attempt to provide an understanding of the course layout. In the absence of a diagram of the course layout, *this work will only ever be the author's best guess*.

One certainty is that some of the holes on the front nine are still in the same location today as they were in 1905. However, holes 8 through to 17 have probably changed quite significantly. The scoring during the exhibition match suggests that the course could not have been much longer than indicated in the table since it was not usual for the top players to break 70 in those days with such apparent ease.

On a final note, the photographs clearly show that the tees and greens were naturally placed. Artificial mounding on a large scale and elevated tees were not a feature of architecture at that time.

Table 2.1

Hole	Length in yards (estimate)	Description	Justification
1	266	Short par 4 - reachable with a good drive	Photograph showing tee marker
2	130	Par 3 - with bunkers both sides and in front	Scores from matches
3	330	Par 4	Author's estimate
4	380	Medium par 4 - similar to hole today.	Author's estimate
		Green in basin short of present green location	Photographs
5	360	Medium par 4 - similar to today with green forward	Photographs - tee, drive bunker
6	130	Par 3 - big bunker in front of green	Photographs
7	440	Short par 5 - similar to the 6th hole today	Author's estimate
8	160	Par 3	Golf Illustrated
9	221	Short par 4 - reachable with a good drive	Golf Illustrated
Out	**2417**		
10	500	Long par 5	Golf Illustrated, Horncastle News
11	102	Shortest par 3	Horncastle News
12	360	Par 4	Author's estimate
13	530	Long par 5 - could be the 14th hole today	Photograph
14	370	Par 4	Author's estimate
15	350	Par 4	Author's estimate
16	150	Par 3	Golf Illustrated
17	230	Par 3	Newspaper report
18	440	Par 5	Newspaper report
In	**3032**		
Out	**2417**		
Total	**5449**	**Par 70**	

Course Developments and Related Events
1905 - 1911

From both media reports and the minutes of the club's AGM, it would appear that there was a clear desire to make regular improvements to the course. It is likely that improvements in golf equipment, particularly the introduction of the rubber cored ball, brought about these changes. This ball could be hit 20 - 30 yards further by golfers of all standards and the course may have been designed with the old 'gutty' in mind. The gutty was preferred by Vardon, who continued to play with it even though he knew he would be at a disadvantage. A quote from *Aspects of Golf Course Architecture 1889-1924* written by Fred Hawtree makes interesting reading: *'We may remember that in 1902, Sandy Herd (307) won the Open at Hoylake by one shot from Vardon (308). Herd on the advice of John Ball was using the new Haskell ball: Vardon was still wedded to the old ball. In the next seven years, a lot of other people's ideas on design changed considerably.'* Views on golf course design were changing at a pace and it seems that changes to the course were made every winter.

The course record of 68 (set at the official opening by both Taylor and Braid) was beaten by the Woodhall Spa professional (A Fosbury) in September 1905 when he scored 67. His front nine was 32 followed by a back nine of 35.

Nisbet's Golf Yearbook of 1911 reported that *'alterations increasing the length were made to the links in 1907.'*

The Lincolnshire Union of Golf Clubs held their annual county championship on May 11th 1908. This was the first time that the new 18 hole course had been used by the LUGC (the event had been held in 1902 on the old nine hole course). Men's and Ladies' championships were held on the same day and on the same course. Defending champion, Miss E C Wilson of Belton Park, won the Gold Medal with a score of 101. Stuart Macrae, also from Belton Park, narrowly beat the holder, J F Wintringham from Cleethorpes, scoring 158 and 159 respectively. As in the exhibition matches in 1905, an analysis of their scores shows that they did not score as well on the back nine as they did on the front nine.

May 21st 1909 edition of *Golfing* reported that *'the Woodhall Spa professional, W. Bowden, is the maker of the Bowden Special rubber cored ball. A splendid 1s 6d ball equal to a good many 2s ones. It drives very well and is good on the greens.'* Bowden was also a respected club maker. In fact, a number of the club's professionals were well known club makers in this era. The photograph (right) shows a collection of clubs, all of which have a connection to Woodhall Spa.

From left to right the clubs are:

1 The 'Giant' Cardinal niblick made by Hendry and Bishop circa 1920 was ordered by Woodhall Spa professional W (Dickie) West (at the Club from 1919 - 33) for the Colonel (apparently so that he could get out of his own bunkers more easily!).

2 An Antishank niblick made by Winton of Montrose for Woodhall Spa professional C L Mothersele (1913 - 15).

3 A Bulger driver with brass base plate made by A Fosbury who was Woodhall Spa professional from 1903 to 1907.

4 A brassie made by W (Dickie) West.

5 A spoon made by W (Dickie) West.

At the Golf Club AGM in 1910, it was reported that a large sum had been spent on the course, including providing water for the greens (stand pipes). Another consistent theme from the Golf Club's AGM minutes was that the Hotchkin family was thanked for making financial, labour and material contributions on an annual basis.

Bernard Darwin refers to Woodhall Spa in his 1910 book of *Golf Courses of the British Isles* (page 141). Discussing Lincolnshire courses, he writes *'...one is Woodhall Spa, which is sandy and heathery and pleasant, with a suggestion of some of the Surrey courses, and not too long and severe for those who come there in order to drink waters and get well.'*

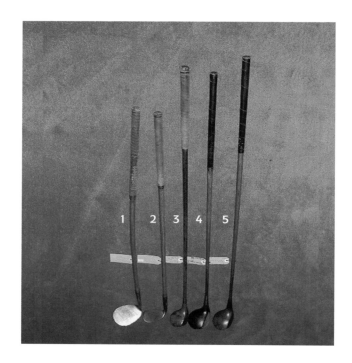

Fire on the course in summer time was also commonplace as sparks from passing trains would often set both the gorse and heather alight. One such fire in 1911 resulted in many people from the town assisting the local firemen to put it out.

On July 1st 1911, it was reported in the *Horncastle News* that a farewell dinner had been held for Stokoe who was retiring after 17 years of service. Stokoe had been such a significant and key figure in the development of the Club and course and no doubt would be missed.

The next major change in course development took place in 1911. On the 3rd June 1911, the *Horncastle News* reported the key points of the Club's AGM. The article states that the Club showed a deficit for the year of £76 2s 10d. S V Hotchkin was thanked for gifts of manure and labour towards the improvement of the course. Due to the financial position, the committee issued a circular regarding the reconstruction of the Club. It stated that a large sum of money had been spent during the past few years on the improvement of the course, and there was unanimous agreement that the present condition of the course justified the expenditure. The expense had indeed been heavy and would not have been possible without the generosity and consideration of the landlord. In order to alleviate the financial position, the Club proposed that: *(a)* a subscription list be opened asking for financial donations to help with the problem *(b)* all members re-joining would be levied one guinea *(c)* members' subscriptions be increased.

Colt's Influence

In the autumn of 1911 and despite the Club's financial situation, it was decided that further improvements to the links should be made. One assumes that the reconstruction plan of the Club's finances had been successful and it was felt that if the course was improved, more visitors would come.

It was agreed that Harry S Colt, the renowned golf course architect and secretary of Sunningdale, should be engaged to advise on course improvements. Colt visited Woodhall Spa in October and stayed for three days, drawing up a full report for the Committee. His charge was £18 and he offered suggestions for changes to all eighteen holes. Work began almost immediately and continued throughout the winter of 1911-12. Once again, the exact details of the changes are not available, but media reports provide enough information to suggest that by 1914, the routing of the course was changed to its present layout. So these changes were therefore particularly significant as new holes were clearly incorporated.

It was reported in the *Horncastle News* that these changes had proved costly, but the dramatic improvement in the course was obvious and it was hoped that these changes would attract more visitors to the course that would also benefit the Spa and the town. This report also mentioned that the changes could not have been achieved without the financial assistance of Mr and Mrs S V Hotchkin. The landlord had waived a £150 rent arrears and made a contribution to the course work of £50 by the end of December 1911. A further contribution of £200 was made in the first part of 1912.

The remaining alterations from Colt's plan were completed in the 1912-13, winter period. During 1912 some valuable suggestions were also received from Ben Sayers and Jack White. In the winter of 1913-14, further small improvements (mainly bunkering) were carried out which completed this important stage of the course development. It was reported that three holes on each nine had been lengthened; the total length of 6,404 yards being 95 yards longer than the course had been the previous year. The 9th hole had been stretched by 24 yards to 540, the 14th measured 500 yards and there were three others well over 400 yards. The bogey was reported as being 80 (41 out and 39 home):

5 5 5 5 3 5 3 5 3 5 **(41)** 4 5 3 5 5 4 4 4 5 **(39)** 80

To commemorate the course improvements, an exhibition match was organised on Saturday 16th May 1914. Ted Ray (Oxley), Tom Ball (Raynes Park), Archie Earl (Lincoln) and C Mothersele (the resident professional at Woodhall Spa) played a strokeplay event in the morning followed by a fourball betterball in the afternoon. Ray won the strokeplay competition with a round of 77. The afternoon match between Ray/Earl and Ball/Mothersele ended all square. Ray commented that *'the extended course was truly magnificent'* and Ball went so far as to say that *'for a pure test of golf the links were the finest in the British Isles, including all the championship courses.'*

Colt's Layout

Colt would have been tasked to make the course a better test of golf. Starting with the Vardon layout, he undoubtedly added length (keeping pace with equipment improvements of that time). The media reported mounding around the greens and clever placement of bunkers. Along with the changes to the routing, one of Colt's legacies would have been the strategic location of key bunkers.

It is likely that Colt's architectural principles* applied to Woodhall Spa would have been:

- to make use of as many natural features as possible
- to develop the land immediately in front of the green
- to place bunkers to test players of all standards. Key bunkers placed strategically to test a golfer's course management
- to design the size and shape of a green in relation to the type of second shot.

As mentioned earlier, the exact record of Colt's improvements to the course could not be found. However, studying old photographs and media reports a picture of the course emerges.

Most significantly, an article printed in *Golf Monthly* in 1912 provides an excellent description of the course: '*The Woodhall Spa course lies over a large tract of sandy heather moorland, and is in many features somewhat similar to Sunningdale. It has the advantage, for a winter course, of being always dry. The holes were laid out with the assistance of Harry Vardon and J H Taylor, and present an excellent test of golf.*

The Committee, being determined that they would have the best possible advice as to improving the course, consulted Mr H S Colt, the eminent golf architect, and he has suggested various alterations and improvements, which have been carried out at great expense.

The Committee have also been fortunate in securing the services of W H White, late of the Edinburgh Mortonhall Golf Club, as head green keeper.

At the first hole, which is a drive or a brassie, there is a big bunker to carry off the tee, with further bunkers guarding the green.

The second is a drive and an iron with the danger of going out of bounds on both sides, and a nice undulating green; while at the third you want a good drive to carry a large punch-bowl green, perhaps the best on the course.

At the fourth, another drive and iron, you must above everything, keep straight; the fifth is a blind one-shot hole of 150 yards, while the sixth is considered by most people to be the best hole on the course. A long straight drive, followed by a long straight brassie, will leave you with a tricky mashie shot to play on to the green, which is large and undulating. The seventh is another one-shot hole on to a green surrounded by trees; the eighth a possible one-shot hole of about 200 yards; and the ninth a good long sporting hole, requiring two full shots and an iron, somewhat similar in character to the sixth.

At the tenth, a drive and a cleek, the going is uphill all the way, with a large sandpit to negotiate in front of the green. The eleventh hole has been lengthened, and at the suggestion of Ben Sayers, Sen., a new green has been made; and the twelfth; two very fine full shots, the green which is saucer-shaped, being well guarded.

The thirteenth is the longest hole on the course. You need a good drive to carry the bunker from the tee, with a good brassie and a full iron to follow. There is a wood all the way on your right to penalize a slice and the green, which is very undulating and tricky, is guarded by well placed bunkers.

A new fourteenth has been made, and the fifteenth lengthened and improved. The sixteenth has also been lengthened and new bunkers made, and otherwise improved. The seventeenth is a very sporting hole of 320 yards, while to get home at the eighteenth you require a well placed drive and a brassie shot, and an accurate mashie on to a large, natural and very sporting green.'

In 1912, the **Horncastle News** had also reported: '...*the magnificent transformation of the course which has been accomplished during the dark months of 1911. The innovations have proved costly, but as an investment they should materialise a veritable gold mine for the club and incidentally for the Spa*'. The report went on to say: '*the course now has new characteristics and from 1 to 18, the holes have been bunkered and hilled up, new greens have been laid with more cute approaches and the course generally made a 'tough 'un'.*' Another interesting comment is how '...*such trenchant changes could have been effected on a course previously so level.*'

The description of the course in **Golf Illustrated** in July 1914 confirmed that the course had undergone further significant changes since 1912, the result being a layout that is similar to that of today: '*From the back tees - two tees, in addition to those for ladies, are kept in use at each hole - the course measures 6,400 yards. The strongest feature, perhaps, are the shots up to the hole and Tom Ball, who recently played an exhibition match with Ray at Woodhall, gives it as his opinion that no better second shots are to be found anywhere. Good driving also receives a great reward, for most of the tee shots require to be perfectly played, and joy shots receive severe treatment from the heather that lines both sides of the fairway. The short holes are also excellent, particularly the 8th, which measures about 170 yards. The shot is played on to a raised green which slopes a little to the right, and at the right hand corner is a deepish pot bunker reminiscent of the notorious Shell bunker at St Andrews. A shot with any suspicion of slice is almost sure to come to rest in this trap, while another big bunker looks after a hook. The fifth is considerably shorter than this and needs an exceedingly accurate shot right on to a slightly hog backed green heavily bunkered on both sides.*

* More information on Colt is given in Appendix One

The bunker to be carried from the third tee is particularly capacious, and a good drive at this hole must be followed by a very accurate iron shot to a fine punch bowl green. The 7th - measuring 394 yards - is a beautiful hole of the dog-leg variety, where a well placed drive leaves a very pretty second which has to be carefully steered to avoid some clever flanking hazards. The 9th is 540 yards long, and unlike the generality of holes over 500 yards, is extremely interesting, being so liberally supplied with big bunkers as to remind one more than a little of Prince's, Sandwich. Cross bunkering has been judiciously utilised at several holes, notably the 11th.'

This description informs us that the holes were now in the same order as today (that is, 5th, 8th and 12th are par 3's etc). It is thought that Colt combined two out of the first three holes of Vardon's layout and made a number of routing changes between the 7th and 15th holes. It would appear that the current 12th hole was also introduced at that time. More bunkers were built introducing some strategic thinking, particularly for shots onto the green. From the information gathered, the yardage of each hole was likely to have been:

1	330	10	310
2	400	11	405
3	385	12	140
4	381	13	409
5	130	14	500
6	460	15	340
7	394	16	350
8	170	17	320
9	540	18	440
Out	**3190**	**In**	**3214**	**Total**	**6404**

Courtesy of Richard Sivill

The 3rd hole

The media reports given on the previous pages illustrate how golf course architecture was changing to keep pace with developments in equipment and the increased interest in the game. Careful consideration was being given to making shots into the green more challenging whilst the placement of hazards was becoming more measured. The penalties for missing the fairway were particularly severe due to the heather and most fairway bunkers were placed laterally. The carries over the heather to many of the fairways were as significant then as they are today.

Course Developments 1914 - 1920

By the time the exhibition match was played between Ball and Ray in June 1914, course alterations had ended. The onset of the First World War clearly was to have an effect although the AGM minutes published in May 1915 reported that income had exceeded expenditure. General upkeep of the course had been the main priority during the 1914-15 winter period. Many prominent members of the Golf Club including Mr Hotchkin joined the armed forces and served their country with honour. Sadly, many did not return.

The AGM minutes of 1916 once again showed that income had exceeded expenditure with a surprisingly large number of green fees taken. The minutes also commented that *'the condition of the course is not as good as usual but members will no doubt take into consideration the difficulties of the present times.'*

During the wartime period, particularly in the latter part, the general maintenance of the playing surfaces would have been the main objective. The effects of war would certainly have taken their toll and interestingly there are references to a 'luxury tax' being

Courtesy of Richard Sivill

The 10th hole

imposed on food served in the clubhouse. Many of the hotels were converted into convalescent homes for wounded soldiers.

The next significant development in the history of the Club and course occurred in 1919. The AGM minutes of June 1919 reported that *'a record season was promised'*, in terms of income. Doctor Williams was presiding over the meeting and he opened by welcoming back Captain Hotchkin*. Captain Hotchkin was thanked for all that he had done for Woodhall Spa and the Golf Club. The minutes also stated that *'if it had not been for him, they would have no club.'* Hotchkin stated that the Club had always received his support and he had every intention of continuing that support in the future. He also said that he was pleased that the prospects of the Club were bright and that the present season promised to be better than ever before. The minutes also reported that the course was returning to its pre-war condition.

The fortunes of the Golf Club must then have taken a severe downturn in the remainder of that year because on the 6th December 1919, an EGM was called *'to consider and confirm an arrangement for the landlord to take over the club as a proprietary one.'* The chairman (Captain Hotchkin) said that the club had not been a financial success and he suggested taking over the links from the committee and making himself responsible for the financial burdens. The members would remain as they were, paying the same subscriptions and with the same privileges, except with regard to tennis. They would have the use of the pavilion, and the benefit of elected officers. However, they would no longer be responsible for the links, and were also relieved of any financial burden. The committee agreed as *'payment of the rent and arrears being too heavy a burden on the resources of the club, there was no other course open.'*

This was certainly a significant chapter in the history of the Golf Club and indeed shaped the future of the course. It is not clear why there was such a change in the fortunes of the Club in six months from the optimistic report given in June. Perhaps the effect of war resulted in less money being available for leisure activities and fewer than expected visitors came to Woodhall Spa. One point that is quite clear from the AGM minutes is that the Hotchkin family had provided the main financial funds for the development of the course since 1905. The rent had been waived on numerous occasions and there had been many other contributions in terms of labour and materials.

By becoming the owner of the Golf Club, Hotchkin then exercised his prerogative in running affairs as he saw fit from 1920 onwards. The minutes of the club ceased to be published in the local press after 1920 as the business was now a private venture. However, Hotchkin's son, Neil, who took over the responsibility of the club in 1953, has confirmed many interesting facts which are covered in the following chapters.

* The 1918 AGM minutes reported that Mr S V Hotchkin, now a Captain in the army (and soon to become a major), had been awarded the Military Cross.

THE HOTCHKIN COURSE – WOODHALL SPA

CHAPTER 3 ~ DEVELOPMENT OF THE COURSE (1920 - 2005)

The course was to undergo one last major development phase before maturing into the present layout. This work was carried by Colonel S V Hotchkin*, who by the early 1920s had developed a considerable interest in golf course architecture. He had worked closely with Vardon in laying out the original eighteen hole course in 1903 and then subsequently with Colt during the re-design work between 1911-14. He had also entertained many top players, exchanging views on course design.

The Colonel's Influence

The Colonel set about making changes to the course in 1922 where, in the first instance, he examined the green complexes and bunkering. He is reported to have re-laid many of the greens, some of which were moved onto new sites. During this early period, course designer and well known amateur golfer, Cecil Key Hutchison offered some advice and ideas. Hutchison was to go into partnership with the Colonel and Sir Guy Campbell at a later date[†].

The Colonel remained true to his architectural principles in the changes he made to Woodhall Spa:

- to present a course of penal nature
- to be bold in bunker design, creating a true hazard essentially through depth
- to relocate and improve the green sites
- to ensure the course remained sympathetic to its natural surrounding
- to create testing green entrances, the width relating to the length of the hole.

These principles were certainly achieved as it is often suggested that Woodhall Spa's bunkers are among the most formidable in the world and the penal nature of the course is well known.

In 1926, the first major event, the English Ladies Championship, was played and the length of the full course was reported to be 6,512 yards.

Alterations to the green sites continued well into the 1930s and it is likely that the 3rd green was one of the last to be moved. The original green used to be in a hollow just short and right of the present green.

From 1926 until his death in 1953, the Colonel added a further 300 yards to the length of the course, continuing to make improvements as when and where he felt necessary.

At the outbreak of the Second World War the Colonel, who at the age of 63 was too old for active service, was determined to at least maintain some form of playing surface. He carried out most of the work himself, with occasional help from an assistant. Perhaps a little ironically given the events unfolding on the world stage, the letter opposite was sent to Club members in November 1939.

During an interview for a golf magazine in the late 1940s, the Colonel was able to state with understandable pride, that since 1920, not one external contractor had been employed on the golf course.

Henry Cotton played an exhibition match at Woodhall Spa in 1940 (raising money for the Red Cross Fund). He commented *'I like the course very much; it can be put down as one of the leading courses in the country of its type, and is an example of what intelligent golf architecture can produce, for looking at some photos of the course taken thirty years ago, I can see that Colonel*

Hotchkin's artistic hand has been very busy making uninteresting flat land into the most natural looking of golf courses.'

---

* Hotchkin had achieved the rank of Major shortly after the end of the war and was to become an Honorary Colonel of the 60th Field Regiment RATA. He became affectionately known as the 'Colonel' and that is how he will be referred to for the remainder of the book.

† More details about the Colonel's life and design principles are given in Appendix One.

Neil Stafford Hotchkin

Neil Hotchkin's Influence

In comparison to his father, the Colonel's son, Neil, was less involved in golf course design. Nevertheless, he staunchly defended his father's architectural principles and worked hard to maintain the course as one of the best in the world. Neil was always aware of the effect that advancements in equipment were having on the course and worked tirelessly to ensure that golfers of the current era faced a similar challenge to those in the past.

It was indeed fortunate that there was enough land available to accommodate new tees, and subsequent changes to the course continued to be generously funded by the Hotchkin family.

In 1954, the English Golf Union chose Woodhall Spa as the venue of the Brabazon Trophy (the English Open Amateur Strokeplay Championship). This was the first of many men's major amateur events to be hosted*. Even though the course could have been an excellent venue for professional events, its infrastructure and location was not ideal. Although some of these issues could have been overcome, the will was not there to make it happen.

In 1959, a large practice ground (300 yards long and a width that varied between 45 and 85 yards) was opened on Good Friday close to the fourth hole. To mark the event, a long driving contest was held. There was an open event for members and visitors and this was won by Lincolnshire County player, G Hopper with a drive of 283 yards. The members' event was won by Lincolnshire County player J W Ellmore, who drove a distance of 254 yards.

In the mid 1960s, a pitch and putt course was laid in 1.6 acres of land adjacent to the clubhouse. Assistance for the design was given by Frank Pennink of C K Cotton and Company. Interestingly, at this time, Neil Hotchkin considered the possibility of building a further nine holes on land that is now the Bracken Course.

Apart from the 18th hole where new tees were built, the design of the course did not alter much until the 1970s. The firm of architects Cotton (CK), Pennink, Lawrie & Partners Ltd were employed to consider some bunker positions and new tee sites. Before setting up his own company, Donald Steel worked for this partnership, and became good friends with Neil Hotchkin.

In July 1971, Tony Jacklin and Tom Weiskopf played Woodhall Spa as a warm up for the Open Championship that was to be played at Royal Birkdale. Weiskopf recorded a 69 to Jacklin's 71. The golf correspondent, Ben Wright, wrote about the game *'Weiskopf had played at Woodhall but once before - 18 months ago in mid-winter. On Thursday he was able to recall every hole with minute accuracy because he regards the course as one of the six best he has ever played. Jacklin has much the same opinion of this truly glorious course. Both men would like to see a watering system on the fairways and greens and for Woodhall to be nominated as the first inland venue for the Open. They know this is hardly a practical proposition because of the shortage of hotels and room for spectators on the course, but it is an intriguing idea.'* A pop-up sprinkler system servicing the greens was installed in the mid 1970s.

Neil Hotchkin consulted Donald Steel on further occasions, in the 1980s and the mid 1990s.[†] One of Donald Steel's observations was that a number of fairway bunkers were now in the heather and he advised that they should be brought more into play. Details are provided in the hole descriptions later in this chapter. At the end of each summer, Neil prepared the winter programme of work, which outlined a continuous programme of minor alterations and refurbishments.

Neil Hotchkin was a quiet, unassuming man who protected his course with huge passion. He was delighted when the course regularly featured high on the list of the world's great courses and always welcomed journalists and golf writers from around the world. His outstanding contribution to amateur golf led to his appointment as President of the English Golf Union in 1972 and of the European Golf Association from 1989 to 1991. In 1995, Neil sold the course and facilities to the English Golf Union with the aim of protecting both the Club and the heritage of the course. When the second course (The Bracken) was built, the original course was named The Hotchkin as a mark of respect to the family. Until his death in February 2004, he still visited the Club on most days and took an active interest in the development of The Hotchkin course.

*A full list is given in Chapter 7

[†] Donald steel was also engaged by the English Golf Union to design the adjoining Bracken Course in 1996.

Layout Comparisons

One major difference between the course in the 1930s and today is the general appearance. Today, trees surround most holes and the gorse and heather are significant hazards. This certainly would not have been the case in the 1930s as views across the course would have been quite open. Some of the photographs incorporated in this chapter clearly illustrate this point, particularly the aerial photographs taken in 1935 and 1963.

In the past, many stories have been written about the course having a bunker for every day of the year. The impression of more bunkers is probably due to the size and depth of the bunkers. Our research has identified only 159 bunkers and whilst it is possible that there may have been a few more, it is most unlikely that there were ever 365. There are in fact 111 bunkers at the current time and this reduction is due mainly to certain bunkers becoming redundant. The bunkers have also become smaller and, in some cases, deeper.

The fairways are slightly narrower today than they were in the 1920s and more shaped. The carries to the fairways from the existing tees have not altered but the introduction of several new championship tees has created longer carries (some of 220 yards). The greens have mostly remained the same with the exception of two that have been levelled and one other that has been renovated.

An estimate of the changes to the length of the course in 1935 compared to today's course is given in **Table 3.1**.

These yardages have been collected from old scorecards and course measurement certificates. It should be noted that measurement equipment and techniques have altered a great deal over the years. In the early days, measurement by chain was

Table 3.1

Hole	1935	1946	1964	1979	1998	2005
1	350	367	358	363	361	361
2	400	414	409	408	442	442
3	408	418	416	417	415	415
4	406	406	407	415	414	414
5	150	154	155	155	148	148
6	500	500	500	506	510	526
7	400	400	412	435	470	470
8	187	195	198	193	192	209
9	540	556	557	560	584	584
Out	3341	3410	3412	3452	3536	3569
10	330	330	331	333	338	338
11	437	445	447	442	437	437
12	144	140	151	152	172	172
13	433	440	438	437	451	451
14	488	500	492	489	521	521
15	321	330	328	325	321	321
16	367	400	400	398	395	395
17	328	330	327	322	336	336
18	465	480	493	516	540	540
In	3313	3395	3407	3414	3511	3511
Total	6654	6805	6819	6866	7047	7080

considered to be the most reliable. At the present time laser and GPS systems are considered to be the most accurate. The author considers the measurements taken in 1946 (taken from a scorecard of Bobby Locke's round during an exhibition match) were particularly inaccurate, judging from scorecards from before and after this date. In the 1998 list, some of the yardages have reduced slightly, due to the adoption of the CONGU recommendation of having 4 yards from the back of a tee to the fixed distance plate.

The main differences are on the 2nd, 6th, 7th, 9th, 12th, 14th,

16th and 18th holes. These holes have been extended without upsetting the balance of the hole. Further details are given later in the chapter.

Changes to the length of the ladies course are given in **Table 3.2**. The yardages show that the course has not altered much in length in recent years which assumes that the ladies who play regularly are content with their challenge. When the English Ladies Championship was played in 2004, the length of the course was 5,900 yards, with some of the holes being played from the men's forward tees.

Table 3.2

Hole	1921	1972	2005
1	305	321	327
2	320	357	351
3	310	371	370
4	328	353	358
5	126	111	113
6	374	412	410
7	322	369	366
8	172	162	164
9	473	463	459
Out	2730	2919	2918
10	243	279	276
11	297	376	372
12	122	116	123
13	384	381	381
14	425	419	420
15	232	291	289
16	305	318	318
17	258	276	280
18	403	394	395
In	2669	2850	2854
Total	5399	5769	5772

1961

THE HOTCHKIN COURSE – WOODHALL SPA

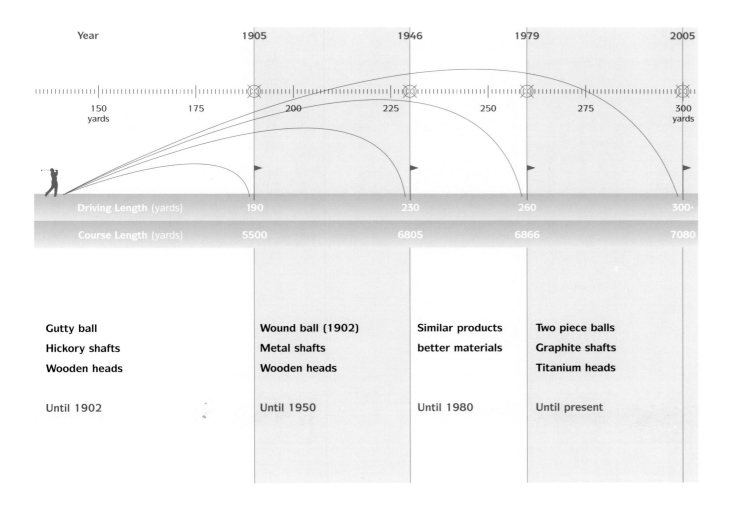

It is estimated that the Vardon layout was in the region of 5,500 yards. By 1914, another 1,000 yards had been added to the course after Colt's recommendations had been implemented. The advent of metal shafts and a better wound ball had resulted in a further 200 yards being added by 1950. Interestingly, there seems to have been little advancement in equipment between 1949 and 1979 which coincides with a period of modest course lengthening. However, the dramatic development in equipment over the last twenty years has seen a further 200 yards being added.

The diagram on this page compares key dates when the course was lengthened with equipment development.

A study into how each hole has changed since 1935 is given in the following pages. The 1935 date has been selected in this study because it is felt that this is the earliest and most reliable layout of the course.

HOLE 1

Development of the 1st Hole from 1935 to 2005

Length/tees

This hole now measures 11 yards longer the 1935 design. The main tee has been extended and enlarged.

Fairway

The fairway width has become narrower and shaped.

Bunkering

The bunkers in front of the tee had become grassy hollows by the mid 1960s. The arrangement of the drive bunkers on the left has gradually altered over the last 80 years and only one remains.
A bunker was added on the right in 1997 (under the supervision of Donald Steel) to make the tee shot more challenging.
The greenside bunkers have been refurbished and reshaped but the locations remain the same.

Green

The green has not been altered.

Flora

Other than a few oak trees on the right, this hole would have been quite open. Over the last 70 years pine, silver birch, oak, gorse and broom surround parts of the hole.

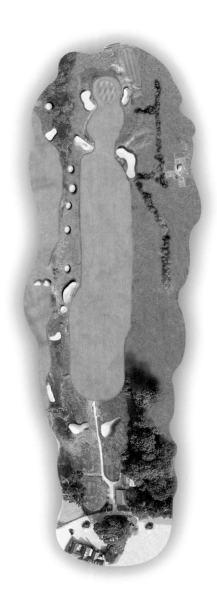

1935 - 350 yards

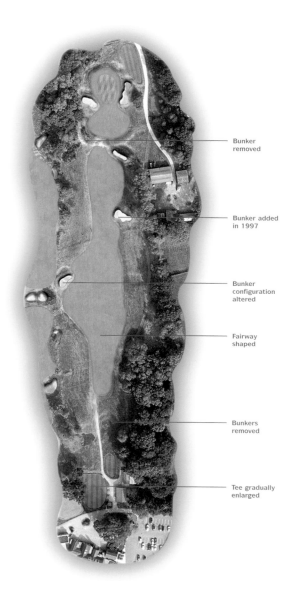

Bunker removed

Bunker added in 1997

Bunker configuration altered

Fairway shaped

Bunkers removed

Tee gradually enlarged

2005 - 361 yards

2nd Hole

1st Hole

1935

1985

HOLE 2

Development of the 2nd Hole from 1935 to 2005

Length/tees

This hole has been lengthened by some 42 yards since 1935. The most significant change came in 1996 when a new championship tee was built, bringing the bunkers on the right more into play.

Fairway

Other than losing some 10 yards in width from the fairway drive bunkers to the green, the fairway remains similar in shape.

Bunkering

The most significant change to the bunkering was the introduction of two other bunkers on the right close to the landing area in the 1970s. In 1989, the two bunkers nearest the fairway were made into one big bunker but returned to their original form in 1999. The two large bunkers some 100 yards short of the green are now heather filled hollows. The bunker short left of the green was split into two in 2000 for maintenance reasons.

Green

The green used to have a dip in the middle running front to back which was reduced in the 1970s.

Flora

In 1935, there would have been very few trees or gorse on the hole compared to how it is today.

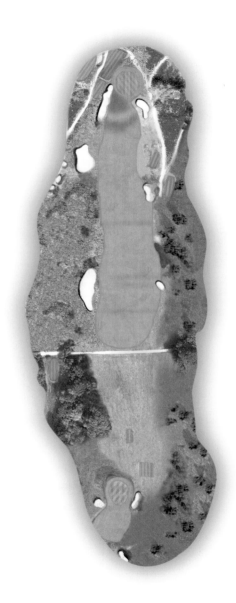

1935 - 400 yards

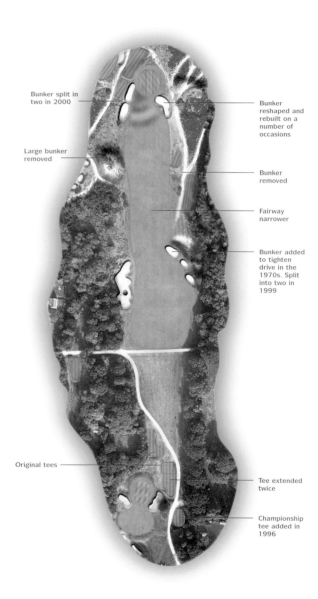

Bunker split in two in 2000

Large bunker removed

Original tees

Bunker reshaped and rebuilt on a number of occasions

Bunker removed

Fairway narrower

Bunker added to tighten drive in the 1970s. Split into two in 1999

Tee extended twice

Championship tee added in 1996

2005 - 442 yards

Clubhouse through the years

1920

1950

1965

1987

HOLE 3

Development of the 3rd Hole from 1935 to 2005

Length/tees

In 1935 this hole would have measured 408 yards. This hole has been lengthened twice by extending the main tee to create a further 7 yards to 415 yards.

Fairway

The carry to the fairway has remained the same but the huge bunker in front of the tee is now a heather filled hollow. The fairway has narrowed slightly but remains the same shape.

Bunkering

The first bunker on the left no longer exists and the left hand bunker arrangement short of the green has been altered to make the green entrance narrower. The right hand green side bunker was originally further to the right than the current position.

Green

The green remains unaltered.

Flora

In 1935 there would have been little gorse and few silver birch trees on this hole. The plantation of fir tees existed but there were fewer of them.

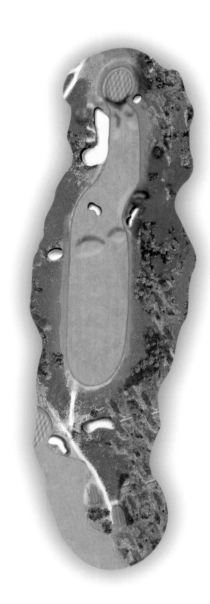

1935 - 408 yards

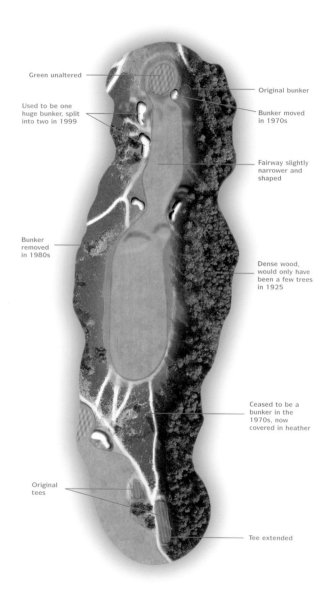

Green unaltered

Original bunker

Used to be one huge bunker, split into two in 1999

Bunker moved in 1970s

Fairway slightly narrower and shaped

Bunker removed in 1980s

Dense wood, would only have been a few trees in 1925

Ceased to be a bunker in the 1970s, now covered in heather

Original tees

Tee extended

2005 - 415 yards

1935

above: Competitors in a ladies event on the 3rd green.

left: This photograph was taken in the early 1950s. The third fairway and fourth fairways can be seen along with a goods train steaming down the track in the distance.

right and above right: The ruined tower beyond the 3rd green, known as Tower on the Moor, is thought to be the remains of a 15th century hunting lodge built by Lord Ralph Cromwell of Tattershall Castle. The tower features on the golf club's logo. The view above right shows a rare shot taken from the top of the tower looking over the 3rd and 4th holes. Today the tower, which is located on private land, is too unsafe to enter.

HOLE 4

Development of the 4th Hole from 1935 to 2005

Length/tees

Slight extension to tee.

Fairway

The carry to the fairway and the width have remained constant.

Bunkering

In 1935, the two bunkers in front of the tee would have seemed quite imposing. In particular, the left bunker was a huge expanse of sand. There was a group of bunkers across the fairway protecting the green from all angles. By the 1960s, these bunkers had been removed and a new left hand drive bunker had been introduced. This bunker was redesigned by Donald Steel in 1997. The bunkers in front of the tee have become smaller and the greenside traps have been redesigned.

Green

The green remains unaltered.

Flora

The appearance of the hole has altered in that there were few trees and gorse bushes even in 1963 (see aerial photograph on page 41). However, there are many gorse bushes surrounding the hole and there is dense copse of trees on the right shielding the practice ground.

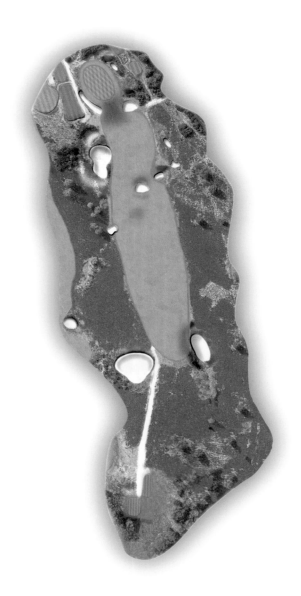

1935 - 406 yards

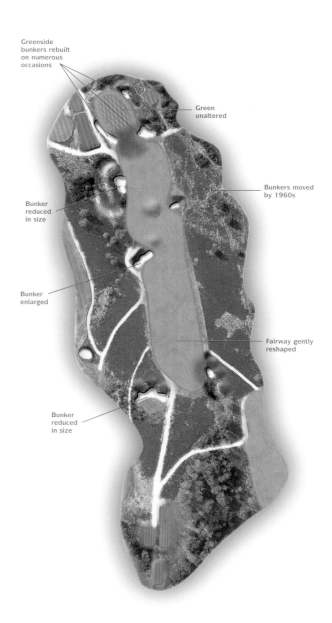

Greenside bunkers rebuilt on numerous occasions

Green unaltered

Bunkers moved by 1960s

Bunker reduced in size

Bunker enlarged

Fairway gently reshaped

Bunker reduced in size

2005 - 414 yards

1963

4th hole

Practice Ground

1985

Interesting Fact

One night after a lengthy practice session, a competitor in the 1974 English Amateur Championship drove his car into the bunker by the side of the fourth green. He thought he would take a short cut back to the clubhouse.

1935

HOLE 5

Development of the 5th Hole from 1935 to 2005

Length/tees

The length remains broadly the same as in 1935. However, new tees have been built to the right of the 4th green to spread wear and tear on the main tee.

Bunkering

Since 1935 the only alteration to the bunkering other than refurbishment work was the removal of a bunker in front of the green.

Green

The green has not been altered.

Flora

In 1935, the green would have been quite open and a clear view of the course and the railway line would have been seen. Today the hole is surrounded by gorse bushes, silver birches (at the back) and broom.

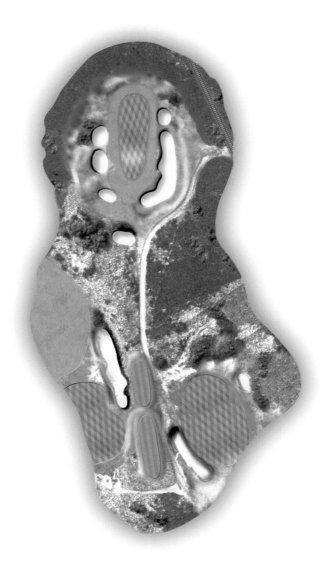

1935 - 150 yards

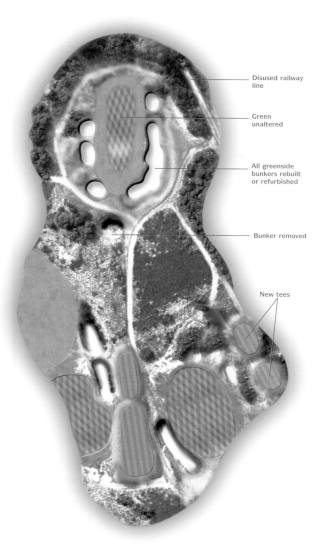

Disused railway line

Green unaltered

All greenside bunkers rebuilt or refurbished

Bunker removed

New tees

2005 - 148 yards

HOLE 6

Development of the 6th Hole from 1935 to 2005

Length/tees

In 1935, this hole would have played as a par 5 measuring 500 yards. The medal tee was extended slightly by 10 yards in the 1980s and a new championship tee was added in 2000.

Fairway

The fairway is slightly narrower now than it was in 1935 but remains similar in shape.

Bunkering

The main alteration to the bunkering is around the green. There used to be a huge expanse of sand on the left running for some 30 yards up to the green side. This has reduced significantly and bunkers no longer exist on the left hand side of the green. However, large gorse bushes now pose a more dangerous threat on the left. The bunker some 150 yards short of the green is now a heather filled hollow.

Green

The green remains unaltered.

Flora

Gorse bushes come into play down the right from the tee and around the green which certainly would not have been there in 1935. Silver birch and pine trees now separate the hole on the left from the 16th fairway. Once again, other than the odd pine tree, this hole would have been completely open.

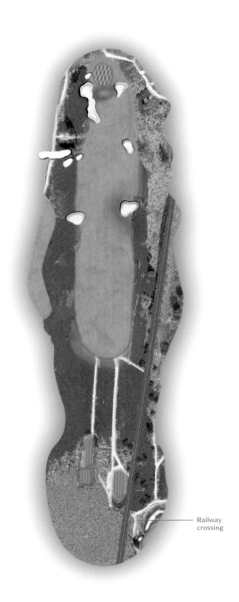

1935 - 500 yards

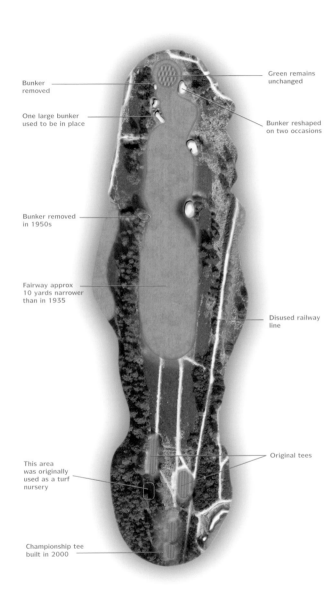

2005 - 526 yards

HOLE 7

Development of the 7th Hole from 1935 to 2005

Length/tees

This hole has increased significantly in length since 1935. The hole would have measured 400 yards and played as a medium length par 4. Various tees have been added to make the drive more challenging as it is possible to cut the corner off the dog-leg from the forward tee. The existing tee was extended by 10 yards in the late 1950s and then a new medal tee was built in the 1970s. The new championship tee added in 1996 stretches the yardage to 470 making a stern challenge. As each new tee has been added the carry to the fairway has been lengthened. From the championship tee the carry is 219 yards compared to 150 yards from the general play tee.

Fairway

The fairway has remained the same.

Bunkering

The bunkering has changed with some bunkers being taken out of play *(see graphics)* and others added - particularly on the dog-leg. These bunkers are strategically placed and have to be carefully negotiated.

Green

The green remains unchanged. However, there used to be some mounds on the left hand side of the green, which were removed in the early 1990s. These mounds used to define the green more clearly when playing the second shot and also prevented shots that were hit slightly left from going into the trees and the gorse.

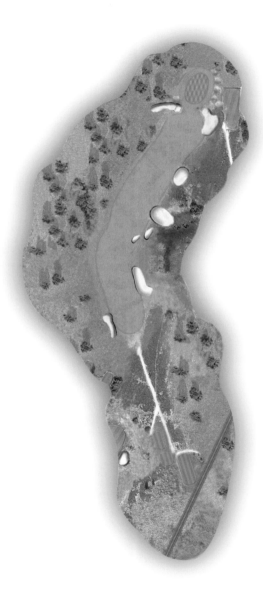

1935 - 400 yards

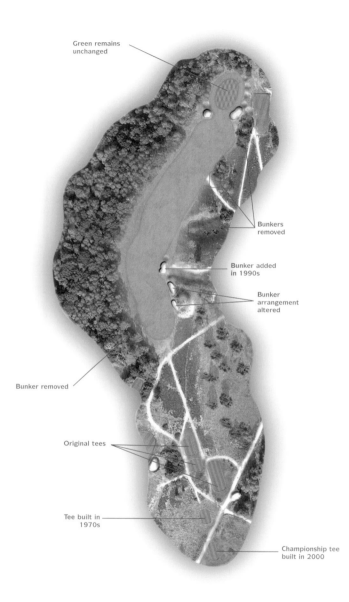

Green remains unchanged

Bunkers removed

Bunker added in 1990s

Bunker arrangement altered

Bunker removed

Original tees

Tee built in 1970s

Championship tee built in 2000

2005 - 470 yards

1930

Flora

Trees now feature heavily on the left hand side of the hole. Although no photographs are available from 1935, careful examination of these trees show that very few would have been there and the adjacent 13th hole would have been seen quite clearly.

Interesting Fact

Silver birch trees and gorse bushes used to grow along the bunker banks down to the corner of the dog-leg. These were removed in 2000 to improve the hole from the championship tee and to return the course to its original form.

HOLE 8

Development of the 8th Hole from 1935 to 2005

Length/tees

This hole has been lengthened twice firstly by extending the original tee in the 1970s and then by adding a new championship tee in 2000. In total, 22 yards has been added bringing the length to 209 yards.

Bunkering

The bunkers have remained in the same position but have been refurbished on a number of occasions. The main alteration has been to split the first greenside bunker on the left into two.

Green

The green has not been altered.

Flora

The main difference is the gorse that has grown and surrounds sections of the hole.

1935 - 187 yards

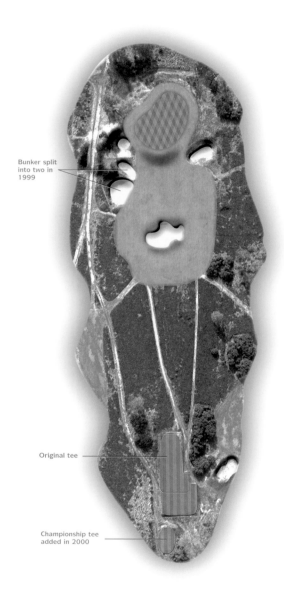

Bunker split into two in 1999

Original tee

Championship tee added in 2000

2005 - 209 yards

Supplied by Simmons Aerofilms Ltd

1963

1985

Interesting Facts

The railway line running down the left hand side of this hole ceased to be used in 1964 when the connection was closed down, undoubtedly as a result of the cuts made to Britain's railway system by Dr Beeching.

An old silver birch tree stands to the left of the 9th tee and level with the 8th green. Embedded in this tree is a golf ball that was driven from the tee about twenty years ago. The bark of the tree has now almost grown over the ball.

HOLE 9

Development of the 9th Hole from 1935 to 2005

Length/tees

This hole now measures about 44 yards longer than in 1935. The original tee has been extended twice - in the 1940s to 555 yards and in 1999 when a new championship tee was built giving a further 29 yards to the length and making the hole the longest on the course at 584 yards.

Fairway

The fairway width has reduced slightly by introducing more semi rough.

Bunkering

In 1935, the right hand drive bunker extended into the fairway and would have been more in the line of play. By the 1960s, this bunker had been reduced in size and, along with the new tee, posed less of a threat with regard to the carry. All but one of the bunkers remain in the same location. The bunker on the right some 50 yards short of the green no longer exists.

Green

The green remains unchanged.

Flora

There was very little gorse or broom on this hole in 1935.

1935 - 540 yards

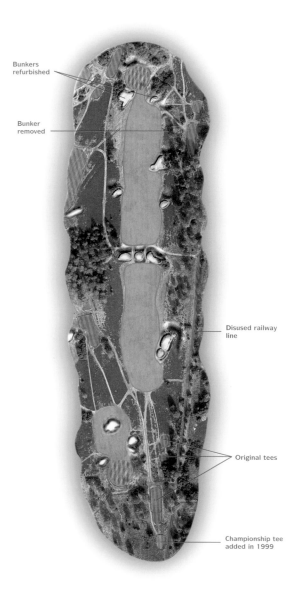

Bunkers refurbished

Bunker removed

Disused railway line

Original tees

Championship tee added in 1999

2005 - 584 yards

Supplied by Simmons Aerofilms Ltd

THE HOTCHKIN COURSE – WOODHALL SPA

HOLE 10

Development of the 10th Hole from 1935 to 2005

Length/tees

The length has not altered much since 1935. The tee has been extended once to add another 8 yards to the hole in 1998. The carry to the fairway remains the same but there would have been a little more room on the right than there is today.

Fairway

The fairway has been reshaped to account for the change in bunkering and is now much narrower in the landing area.

Bunkering

The most significant change to this hole was the addition of a drive bunker on the left hand side in 1998. There used to be one in a similar location (see 1935 aerial photograph) but this was removed in the 1960s. The configuration of the greenside bunkers has changed slightly during a recent refurbishment in 1997. The left hand greenside bunkers have been reduced to two and the right hand bunker has now also been split into two.

Green

The green remains unaltered.

Flora

In 1935, this hole would have been completely open. The aerial photograph shows the fairway bunker arrangement and the close proximity of the railway track.

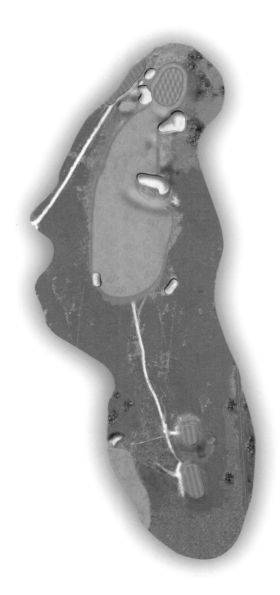

1935 - 330 yards

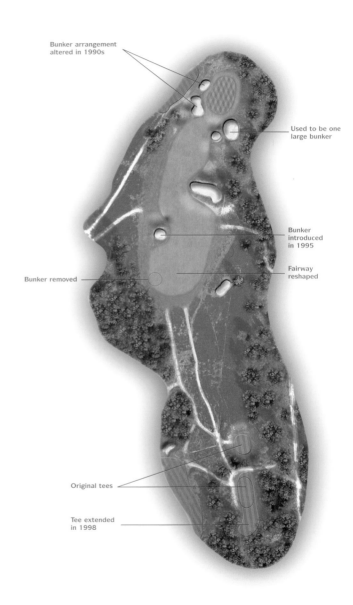

Bunker arrangement altered in 1990s

Used to be one large bunker

Bunker introduced in 1995

Bunker removed

Fairway reshaped

Original tees

Tee extended in 1998

2005 - 338 yards

1935

1985

Supplied by Simmons Aerofilms Ltd

1963

HOLE 11

Development of the 11th Hole from 1935 to 2005

Length/tees

No alteration to the length.

Fairway

The fairway is approximately 10 yards narrower today than in 1935 and similar in shape.

Bunkering

The right and left hand drive bunkers are now grassy hollows and the cross bunkers were made into one in 1999 during refurbishment.

Green

The green remains unaltered.

Flora

In 1935, this hole would have looked dramatically different. The fir trees on the right would have been small and there would have been few trees behind the green. The dense copse on the left would almost certainly have not been there, as the photograph of the 12th green (see next hole) taken in the early 1920s illustrates.

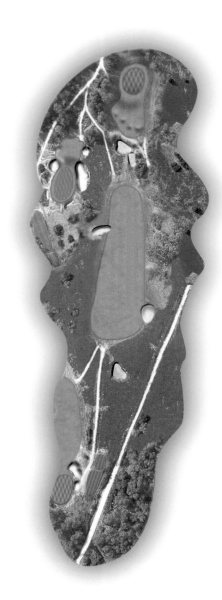

1935 - 437 yards

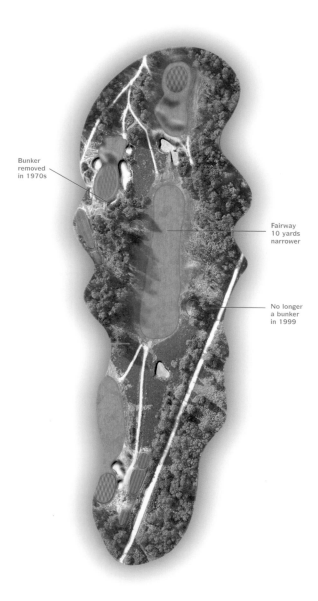

Bunker removed in 1970s

Fairway 10 yards narrower

No longer a bunker in 1999

2005 - 437 yards

Interesting Facts

The Scots Pines on the right hand side of this hole were probably planted around 1914. Today they stand very tall although some were lost during the gales in 2000 and 2001. Replacements have been planted.

A public footpath known as 'The Viking Way' runs through the course crossing holes 11, 12, 13 and 15. This footpath measures 130 miles between Oakham in the south and Barton-upon-Humber in the north. The idea of a long distance footpath in Lincolnshire was the brainchild of John Hedley Lewis, a former Chairman of the County Council and keen walker, who died in 1976. The following year, The Viking Way was officially adopted by the three neighbouring counties of Lincolnshire, Humberside and Leicestershire.

The Viking Way, which could also have been named 'The Lincolnshire Way', crosses through an area that the Danes occupied for many years around 800AD and it was felt that the name was justified.

HOLE 12

Development of the 12th Hole from 1935 to 2005

Length/tees

This hole measured 144 yards in 1935 and was gradually extended to 151 by the 1980s. In 1997, the length was extended to 172 yards when a raised tee was built behind the main tee. In 2002, it was decided to lower the championship tee back to the height of the normal tee essentially to produce more teeing ground and to ease maintenance.

Bunkering

The bunkering around this hole has been altered dramatically. The three bunkers short of the green have been allowed to grow over as they no longer present a hazard and the bunkers around the green have been refurbished and deepened. In 2000, the bunker on the left was rebuilt incorporating a revetted face which is approximately 12 feet high. The bunker on the front right has also been rebuilt in a similar manner presenting a sterner challenge.

Green

The green has not been altered.

Flora

The appearance of this hole changed dramatically from how it looked in 1935. Standing on the tee, a clear view of the signal box behind the 10th green could be seen. A wood, some 150 yards long, now obscures this view and the green has a backdrop of silver birch, pine and gorse. Trees now also obscure the 11th and 13th holes and the tee.

1935 - 144 yards

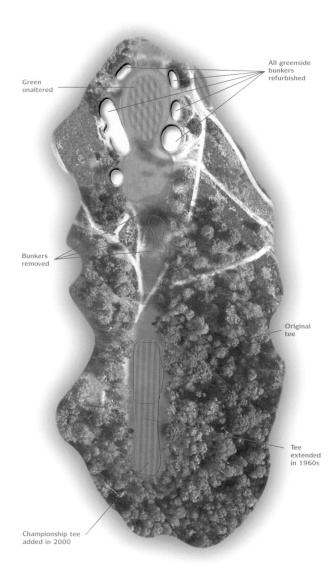

Green unaltered

All greenside bunkers refurbished

Bunkers removed

Original tee

Tee extended in 1960s

Championship tee added in 2000

2005 - 172 yards

1920

1930

MARCH 11 1982
PLAYING A SINGLES MATCH
L.D. HENSHAW HOLED IN ONE
J.A. WILSON HOLED OUT FOR A HALF

1930

1985

Interesting Facts

During a club knockout match in 1982, incredibly two members halved the hole in one. A commemorative plaque has been placed by the tee.

A competitor in the 2000 Brabazon Trophy endured a tough experience when playing the 12th. In his second round he was one over par for the championship before playing this hole and 13 over par when he completed it! He managed to hole out in 15 after a few difficult moments in the left hand bunker.

HOLE 13

Development of the 13th Hole from 1935 to 2005

Length/tees

This hole has been gradually lengthened by extending the tee backwards. In the 1970s, the hole was extended by a further 18 yards. In 1998, the back portion of the tee was raised slightly to give a better view of the fairway.

Fairway

The carry to the fairway from the original tees has not altered and other than a little shaping and a narrowing of about five yards, the fairway remains the same.

Bunkering

In 1935, there were six drive bunkers - three short of the fairway, two on the left and one on the right. Only two of the original bunkers remain although a further bunker was added on the right in the 1980s. The bunker arrangement nearer the green has also been altered making the cross bunkers more challenging. The two greenside bunkers no longer exist.

Green

The green has been altered quite significantly by removing a large tier about two thirds up the green.

Flora

There would have been fewer trees in 1935 and the left hand side of the hole would have been quite open. The wood on the right would have been sparse.

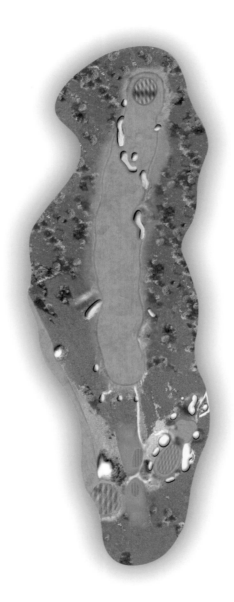

1935 - 433 yards

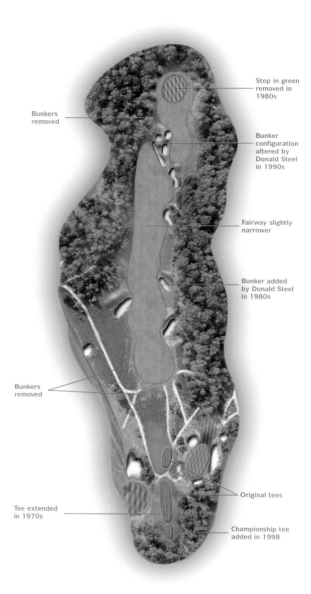

Step in green removed in 1980s

Bunkers removed

Bunker configuration altered by Donald Steel in 1990s

Fairway slightly narrower

Bunker added by Donald Steel in 1980s

Bunkers removed

Original tees

Tee extended in 1970s

Championship tee added in 1998

2005 - 451 yards

HOLE 14

Development of the 14th Hole from 1935 to 2005

Length/tees

The hole has been lengthened by 33 yards since 1935. The current championship tee was built in the early 1990s.

Fairway

The carry to the fairway has remained the same. The fairway itself has been shaped and is at least 10 yards narrower than the original design. Most of this width has been lost on the right hand side where there is clear evidence of bunkers where trees and gorse now grow.

Bunkering

The right hand drive bunkers have been reshaped but the most significant change has been the removal of the cross bunkers which could have been reached from the original tees. The bunkers on the right hand side no longer exist and the most important strategic change (by Donald Steel in 1989) was bringing the left hand bunker, some 50 yards short of the green, more into play.

Green

The green remains unaltered.

Flora

The encroachment of silver birch trees and gorse has undoubtedly changed the character of this hole over the years. The plantation on the right hand side beyond the boundary fence existed before the golf course was built but it is likely that the hole was quite open with few trees on the left hand side.

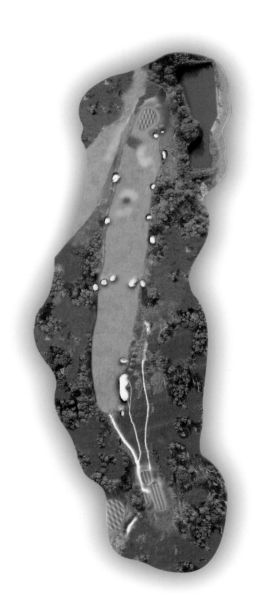

1935 - 488 yards

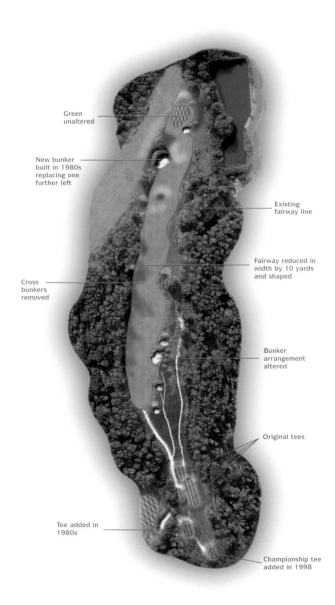

Green unaltered

New bunker built in 1980s replacing one further left

Existing fairway line

Fairway reduced in width by 10 yards and shaped

Cross bunkers removed

Bunker arrangement altered

Original tees

Tee added in 1980s

Championship tee added in 1998

2005 - 521 yards

HOLE 15

Development of the 15th Hole from 1935 to 2005

Length/tees

The length of the hole and the teeing ground remain unaltered.

Fairway

The fairway has narrowed slightly and is more shaped.

Bunkering

The two right hand drive bunkers used to be one large bunker - this change was introduced in 1998. There used to be a bunker some 50 yards short and right of the green but this no longer exists. The greenside bunker arrangement have altered as shown on the graphics.

Green

The green remains unaltered.

Flora

Trees would always have been a feature on this hole but there would have been far fewer in 1935. Gorse and silver birch have grown in abundance and now surround the green as well as the fairway.

1935 - 321 yards

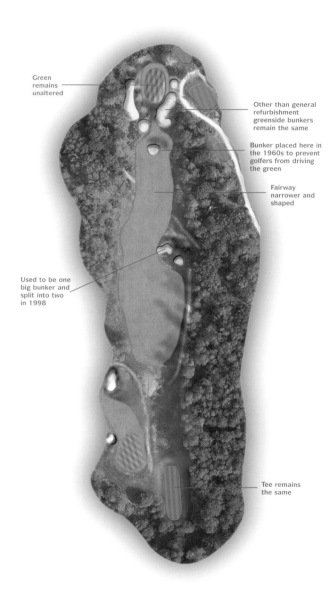

Green remains unaltered

Other than general refurbishment greenside bunkers remain the same

Bunker placed here in the 1960s to prevent golfers from driving the green

Fairway narrower and shaped

Used to be one big bunker and split into two in 1998

Tee remains the same

2005 - 321 yards

HOLE 16

Development of the 16th Hole from 1935 to 2005

Length/tees

A new championship tee had been added by 1950 increasing the length to 395 yards.

Fairway

The carry to the fairway remains the same but the fairway is narrower now by at least 10 yards compared to the width in 1935.

Bunkering

The 1935 design featured six bunkers on this hole. Today only one remains, the others having been allowed to grow over.

Green

This green used to have a tier at the back. The green was levelled in the 1980 s and gravel banding used in 1997 to improve drainage.

Flora

This hole would have looked quite open in 1935 as there would have been fewer trees, particularly on the left.

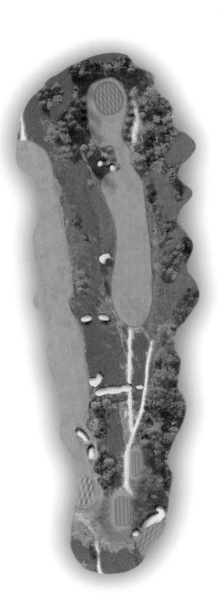

1935 - 367 yards

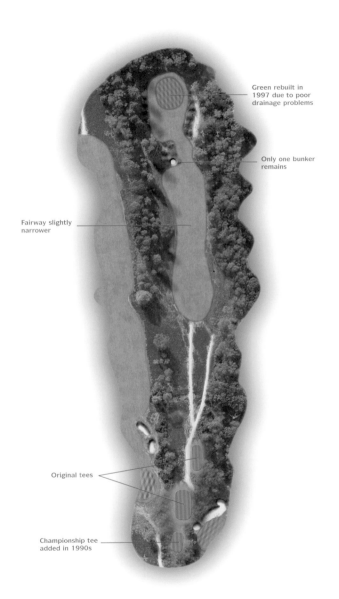

Green rebuilt in 1997 due to poor drainage problems

Only one bunker remains

Fairway slightly narrower

Original tees

Championship tee added in 1990s

2005 - 395 yards

HOLE 17

Development of the 17th Hole from 1935 to 2005

Length/tees

The original tees are shown on the above diagram and the back tee was extended by 8 yards by 1990.

Fairway

The fairway remains the same although reduced in width by about 5 yards.

Bunkering

The main difference from the original design to now, is the removal of the cross bunkers in front of the tee. The greenside bunkers have been refurbished and right hand greenside bunker was completely redesigned by Donald Steel.

Green

The green remains unaltered.

Flora

This hole has not changed that much as the photograph shows. Unlike other holes, trees did feature on this hole and the similarity is quite surprising compared to other parts of the course.

1935 - 328 yards

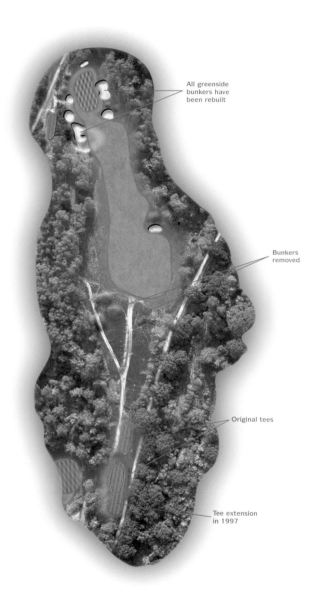

All greenside bunkers have been rebuilt

Bunkers removed

Original tees

Tee extension in 1997

2005 - 336 yards

Interesting Fact

In 1935, the 17th hole was considered by many who played the course to be one of the most challenging, even though it was short in length. The Colonel was asked by a local newspaper to write a description:

'It may seem a simple matter to write a description of what is considered to be the most difficult hole on this course. But I should like to make it clear that this is by no means the case. It may seem insulting to numbers of other holes to pick one out of many. But there seems to be a consensus of opinion that the seventeenth hole should be the one selected. This is so because many golfers, through over anxiety, have sealed their fate there. I have seen this happen even during some of the final rounds of a championship.

This hole is a semi dog-leg from right to left; there is a path and wood ditch on the right, and birch trees on the left, and a large cross bunker to carry 145 yards from the tee. To those who slice there is a mound with a bunker in the face, and those who pull will find themselves in the bonny purple heather.

The feature of the hole is that a long drive is necessary to make the shot easier for a difficult approach, and this should be played to the right of the fairway to open up the hole. Should the drive be played to the left of this fairway, the approach is exceptionally difficult, as on the left of the green, which protects and covers the left side of the green.

There is a narrow entrance sloping from left to right into a sand hollow on the right entrance of the green, and should a shot be played not sufficiently near the bunker on the left, or not firmly enough, into the bunker on the right you will go. Should you attempt to pitch on the green, which is a good size, a slice will send you down a bank into a bunker on the right of the green; if the shot is too strong, you will find yourself in a deep grass hollow. Like many good holes, if you are playing it well you think how simple it is, but should you once find trouble and then lose your nerve, it may veritably develop into your golfing nightmare. Naturally the only course open to those who have doubts whether the seventeenth is the most difficult hole on the course is for them to come and find out for themselves.'

HOLE 18

Development of the 18th Hole from 1935 to 2005

Length/tees

The length of this hole has changed on a number of occasions over the last 70 years. A championship tee was built specifically for the Brabazon Trophy in 1954 which not only lengthened the hole to a par 5 of 490 yards, but changed the hole from a slight dog-leg to straight. At the same time, a general play tee on the same line was added to spread the wear and tear on the main tee. In the late 1970s, a new championship tee was installed level with the 17th green. This proved to be a successful site and in 1989, the hole was extended by building another championship tee further back on the same line, achieving a length of 540 yards.

Fairway

The carry to the fairway altered when the new championship tee was introduced and the fairway was extended back by some 25 yards in the 1970s. The fairway has not altered much in width but was split into two distinct sections in the 1990s when it was decided to let rough grow around the cross bunkers.

Bunkering

The bunkering has not altered much over the years other than general refurbishment and the splitting of the left hand greenside bunkers into two. The greenside bunker on the right and a fairway bunker that used to be short of the fairway on the right no longer exist. The bunker some 70 yards short of the green on the left has been enlarged and brought into play more.

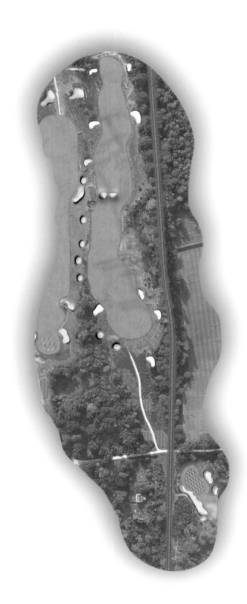

1935 - 465 yards

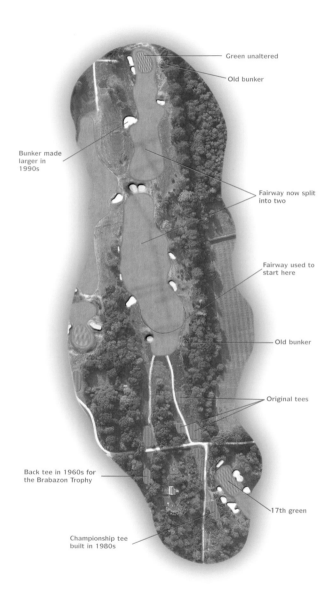

Green unaltered

Old bunker

Bunker made larger in 1990s

Fairway now split into two

Fairway used to start here

Old bunker

Original tees

Back tee in 1960s for the Brabazon Trophy

17th green

Championship tee built in 1980s

2005 - 540 yards

Green

The green remains unaltered.

Flora

Like the 17th hole, there has been little change. The trees on the right are over 100 years old and, other than some gorse bushes, the view is the same. There used to be a large oak tree on the left some 170 yards short of the green but that was lost during a storm in the 1970s. Another oak has self-seeded in close proximity to the original tree site and three oaks on the other side of the fairway have been planted.

Interesting Fact

In the 1978 Brabazon Trophy, the leader hooked his tee shot from the 18th tee - his ball coming to rest on the 1st fairway. He had a clear shot to the green and went on to win the championship. It was decided to plant a copse of trees between the two fairways at this point to punish future hooked tee shots. Only three trees have survived but gorse and broom now fill that area.

1998

THE HOTCHKIN COURSE – WOODHALL SPA

The Hotchkin course at Woodhall Spa is one of the world's classic heathland courses. Very few courses in this category are considered better and it has been repeatedly featured in the various lists of the world's top courses. In November 2002 and 2004, *Golf World* magazine voted The Hotchkin as the best inland course in England and ninth and tenth respectively out of all courses in the UK. *Golf Magazine of America* (widely regarded as the definitive list and last published in 2003) voted The Hotchkin as the 46th best course in the world.

Geology of Woodhall Spa

The course was laid out on a long narrow tract of sandy land. By contrast, the adjoining Bracken Course, which opened for play in 1998, is on clay. The reason for the difference is the effect of glaciation on this part of Lincolnshire. Around 200,000 years ago, ice sheets spread from the north across the whole of eastern England, and when they melted, a thick veneer of boulder clay was left covering most of central Lincolnshire. Then, after a warmer period and about 25,000 years ago, the ice advanced again from Scotland and Scandinavia. It jammed against the eastern edge of the Wolds and blocked off the Humber estuary and what is now The Wash. The whole of Lincolnshire effectively became a vast lake.

During the summers, meltwater rushed down the Bain valley from the tundra-like Wolds and spread a large delta of flinty gravel and sand into the edge of the lake. When the ice finally melted and unblocked The Wash gap, the lake drained away, the delta dried out and fine sands were blown into dune-like features. Vegetation began to colonise the acid soils and then, as the climate became warmer, trees (particularly birch) and rhododendrons spread, to give today's mosaic of heathland wildlife habitats.

It so happens that the boundary between the earlier glacial boulder clay and the edge of the delta of outwash sands and gravels runs through the two courses. Most of The Hotchkin course is on sand and gravel, except holes 14, 15 and 16 and parts of 7 and 17 which are on boulder clay, as is the whole of the Bracken Course (see diagram on next page).

Water logging of areas of the shallower sand cover led to an aggregation of iron minerals on the water table and the creation of an impervious iron pan, or 'ozen' as it is known locally. This is characteristically one foot to four feet below the surface, although there are occasional vertical lumps. When trees were planted during course construction, the pan had to be broken to allow their roots to reach the present day water table below.

Being built on the sandy part of the former delta, The Hotchkin course drains exceptionally well, making it firm and fast running in summer and ideal for play in winter. Such is its variety of habitat that in 1967, the entire course with the exception of the 1st and 18th holes was designated by English Nature as a Site of Special Scientific Interest (SSSI).

Architecture

In architectural terms, golf courses can be broadly classed into the three design categories: **strategic**, **penal** and **heroic**. A **strategic** hole can be defined as one that can be played successfully in a number of different ways balancing risk and reward. For example, a golfer may elect to hit his ball close to a well placed hazard to achieve a better line to the green. A **penal** hole is defined as one where the only way to the target is to carry a particular hazard. Finally, a **heroic** hole is really a combination of the previous two where the more a golfer takes on a particular hazard, the greater the reward. However, it would also be possible to play the hole in a cautious manner to avoid most of the hazard.

The Hotchkin course falls mainly into the penal category even though some of the holes could be regarded as strategic. This is because there are 12 holes where a significant carry over heather to reach the fairway is required. The penalties for missing the fairway (in terms of various hazards - gorse, trees and heather) are severe and compounded by the severity of both the fairway and greenside bunkers. Whilst the penal definition sounds a harsh description, it must be remembered that some of the best courses in the world (Pine Valley, for example) are considered to be in this category.

Respite is given in the form of generous fairways, although they do appear narrower because of the heather and gorse. The main hazards on the course are the bunkers which are world renowned both for their depth and their size. Compared with modern courses, the fairway bunkers are real hazards; in most cases the greens cannot be reached from them.

The general design is uncomplicated and the golfer's qualities of strength, accuracy and finesse are all required.

Layout/Routing

The course has a similar routing to that of a links course - 9 holes out and 9 holes back. The 10th green is, in fact, the furthest point from the clubhouse. The distance between green and tee on most holes is minimal and excellent use of the natural features of the site have been made.

The prevailing wind is predominantly from the west which essentially means that six holes on the front nine are down wind and six on the back nine are into wind.

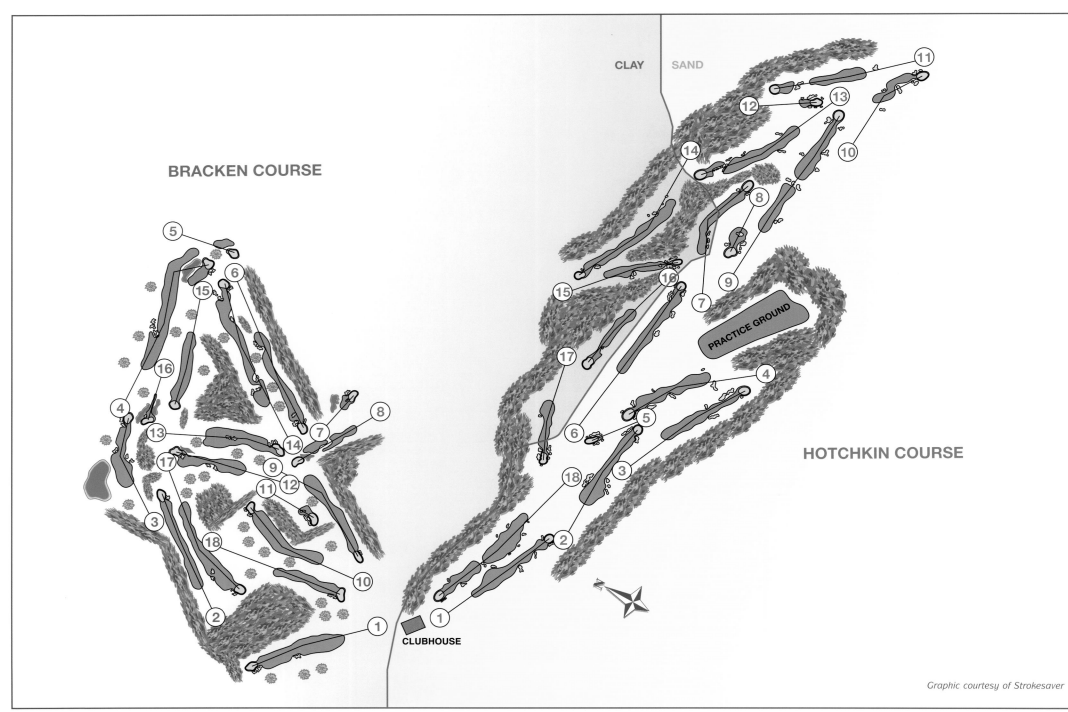

BRACKEN COURSE

HOTCHKIN COURSE

CLAY   SAND

PRACTICE GROUND

CLUBHOUSE

Graphic courtesy of Strokesaver

Psychology of Design

The reputation of The Hotchkin course is one of deep bunkers and tight fairways that make it a tough challenge for golfers of all standards. There is no doubt that the bunkers are deep and can be difficult to play from but the fairways are quite generous (30 - 35 yards in most cases). The heather definitely focuses the mind because there is an immediate visual penalty for missing the fairway compared perhaps to one that is surrounded by rough. Hence, the architect has managed to make the course look harder from the tee than it actually is.

Development in equipment has ironically introduced a strategic element on some of the holes. The golfer is enticed to hit past the fairway bunkering on some holes, but the risk versus reward option has to be carefully considered.

There are four short par 4's which provide some relief from the longer holes. However, these holes can be 'card wreckers' if the golfer loses concentration.

There are only three par 3's and the penalties for missing the green on each of them is very severe. Two of the holes (5th and 12th) appear almost as island greens and can cause the golfer to be distracted by the severity of their appearance.

The use of 'dead ground' has been used extremely well on some holes, particularly the 2nd, 10th and 11th. The architect has managed to trick the golfer into thinking that the green is closer than it actually is.

Balance

At the time of writing, the course measures 7,080 yards from the championship tees. Both nines are similar in length (front - 3,569 yards, back - 3,511).

There are three par 3's, eleven par 4's and four par 5's:

Par 3's

Two are on the front nine and one on the back nine

Length - short (148 yards), medium (172 yards) and long (209 yards)

Par 4's

Four short par 4's - under 370 yards (one on the front nine, three on the back nine)

Three medium par 4's - 370 yards to 420 yards (two on the front nine, one on the back nine)

Four long par 4's (two on each nine)

Par 5's

Two on each nine (two medium and two long)

Of the par 4's and 5's, eight are straight holes, two dog-leg holes to the left and five dog-leg holes to the right.

Placement of Hazards

Bunkers

At the time of writing, there are 111 bunkers on the course in total. The following table shows the bunker distribution.

There are 34 fairway bunkers on the right as opposed to 18 on the left, posing a danger to those golfers who tend to hit the ball left to right.

Trees

Trees that affect the tee shot are on the 3rd, 6th, 7th, 11th, 13th, 14th, 16th, 17th and 18th holes. Trees that affect the approach shot are on 11th, 14th, 16th and 18th holes. In particular, a large single oak on the 18th hole placed on the right severely effects the second shot if the drive finishes right of centre. The well known American architect, **Tom Doak**, uses this hole as an example in his book '**The Anatomy of a Golf Course**'. He writes 'Trees may also be used as a strategic hazard, where the tree is clearly healthy and as long as some latitude is given for the tree to grow without the hole changing considerably. A simple example is the 18th hole at Woodhall Spa, England. A huge oak tree on the right about 170 yards from the green means the tee shot must be kept to the left of the fairway to have a clear line to the green with the second shot, yet the green can still be reached after a wayward drive if the second shot is dramatically faded around the tree. The tree is perfectly located midway between the landing area and green. When trees are too close to the landing area, the difference between having a clear shot to the green or no shot at all rests more heavily on the matter of luck.' These are excellent words of advice and the oak tree on the 18th still provides a wonderful strategic hazard.

Bunker Placements	1	2	3	4	5	6	7	8	9	10	11	12	13	14	15	16	17	18	Total
Fairway bunkers left	1	1	2	3	-	1	-	-	1	1	-	-	1	1	-	1	-	5	18
Fairway bunkers right	2	3	1	2	-	2	3	-	4	2	1	-	4	4	2	-	1	3	34
Cross bunkers	-	-	-	-	-	-	-	3	-	1	-	3	-	-	-	-	-	2	9
Greenside bunkers left	1	2	1	1	3	1	1	3	1	2	-	3	-	-	2	-	3	2	26
Greenside bunkers right	1	1	1	2	2	1	1	1	1	2	-	3	-	1	2	-	2	-	21
Greenside bunkers short	-	-	-	-	-	-	1	-	-	-	-	-	-	-	1	-	-	-	2
Greenside bunkers long	-	-	-	-	-	-	-	-	-	-	-	-	-	-	-	-	1	-	1
Total																			111

Green Size

The greens are predominantly flat and vary in length from 28 to 36 yards.

Green Entrances

Green entrances vary between 6 and 24 yards wide. This is quite narrow compared to many courses but consistent with the overall penal design principles.

Landing Areas

Most of the intended landing areas are reasonably wide (25 - 35 yards) and are predominantly flat.

Course Preparation

In normal summer conditions, the greens are mown to a height of 4.5mm, tees and approaches at 10mm, fairways at 14mm, and semi-rough at 38mm. The ultimate aim of the greenkeeping staff is to present the course on a daily basis in a similar condition to that of when a tournament is being played.

THE HOTCHKIN COURSE – WOODHALL SPA

CHAPTER 5 ~ PLAYING THE COURSE

This chapter provides a description of how to play The Hotchkin course on a hole by hole basis, supported by a collection of photographs taken from the tee and the ideal position on the fairway.

In simple terms, once a site has been examined taking into consideration the natural features, the golf course architect will lay out the course focusing on how a scratch golfer would play the course. Further tees are then placed to ensure that the higher handicap golfer is presented with a fair test.

The hole descriptions given in this chapter aim to present a clear picture of how the course should be tackled. Golfers of varying skills and abilities will also perhaps appreciate a little about course management by taking note of key architectural features. Photographs from the tee have been taken and the ideal line is indicated along with hazards that come into play. Similarly, a view of the second shot has been provided along with green information.

A broad appreciation of the intentions of the golf course architect will undoubtedly assist any golfer wishing to improve their game and will increase the enjoyment of playing the world's great golf courses.

The Hotchkin course at Woodhall Spa is a classic heathland course. Built on sand, the course is generally dry in winter and fast running in summer. The flora and fauna are typical of a lowland heathland course - gorse, broom, bracken, heather and silver birch abound the fairways and the wildlife have a wonderful natural habitat in which to thrive.

There are only three par 3's but each varies in length and present tremendous challenges. The Hotchkin course is famous for its bunkers and it is arguably the only course in the world that has

so many deep hazards. The land made available for the golf course at the time of building was long and fairly narrow (and bisected by a railway line) which led to typical links layout - 9 holes out and 9 holes back.

The red arrows on the diagram indicate the prevailing wind direction. This is an important factor as Lincolnshire is a predominantly flat county and therefore susceptible to strong winds.

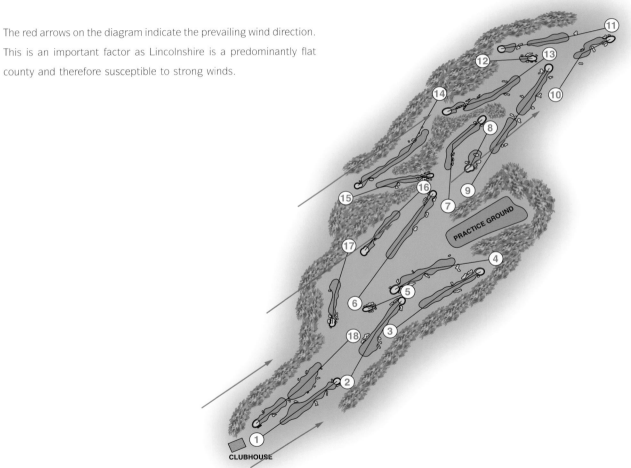

THE HOTCHKIN COURSE – WOODHALL SPA

HOLE 1

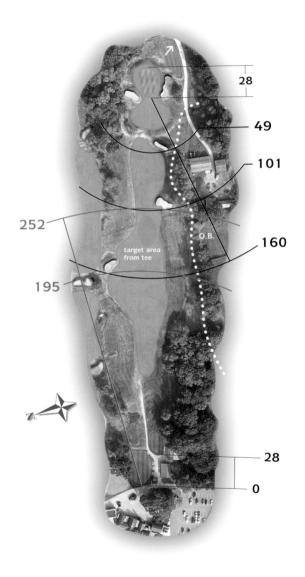

The first hole of this classic championship course is a generous opener, designed to allow play to proceed quickly. It is a short par 4 requiring strategic play from the tee.

Championship Tee

HOTCHKIN COURSE
1
361 YDS
−330 MTRS−
PAR S.I.
4 ● 17
WOODHALL SPA

Medal Tee

HOTCHKIN COURSE
1
361 YDS
−330 MTRS−
PAR S.I.
4 ● 17
WOODHALL SPA

Yellow Tee

HOTCHKIN COURSE
1
353 YDS
−322 MTRS−
PAR S.I.
4 ● 17
WOODHALL SPA

Ladies Tee

HOTCHKIN COURSE
1
327 YDS
−299 MTRS−
PAR S.I.
4 ● 17
WOODHALL SPA

The Tee Shot (long iron or fairway wood)

From the main tee the golfer can see all before him. The ideal line is just left of the right drive bunker, shown clearly in the photograph. There are two bunkers in play from the tee: one left at a distance of 195 yards from the back tee and another at 251 yards on the right. It is the right hand drive bunker that is undoubtedly feared the most. The prevailing wind is behind on this hole and when the fairways are firm, this bunker can easily be reached. The landing area is generous (39 yards) but narrows significantly to 20 yards the further the tee shot is struck.

Bunker at 195 yards

Bunker at 251 yards

VIEW FROM THE 1ST TEE

The Second Shot

From the centre of the fairway, the second shot is normally a short iron. Two bunkers are situated left and right. The bunker on the left hand side is deeper than the one on the right. Compared to most other greenside bunkers on the course, these are fairly shallow.

The Green

The green is 28 yards long and has two small ledges on the left and at the back. Although predominantly flat, the green tilts slightly from back to front and there are more pronounced breaks on the left hand side.

Green Complex

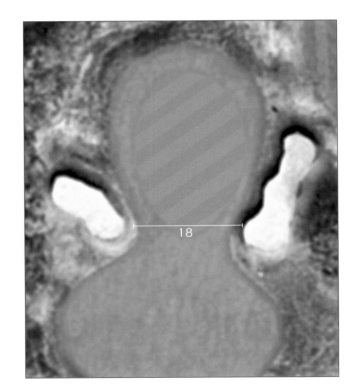

THE HOTCHKIN COURSE – WOODHALL SPA

HOLE 2

A long straight par 4 hole, played slightly uphill to a green that is heavily guarded by bunkers. A strategic decision is required from the tee.

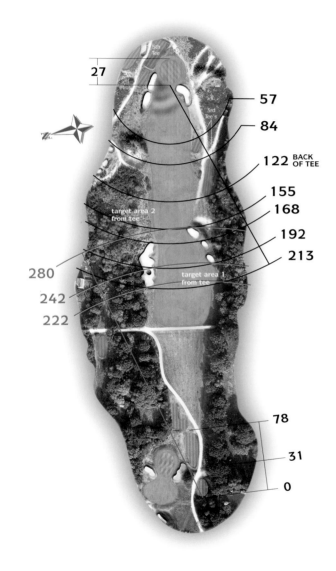

Championship Tee

Medal Tee

Yellow Tee

Ladies Tee

The Tee Shot (driver or long iron/fairway wood)

Like the first hole, the prevailing wind is normally behind and whilst the hole is quite straight, club selection is dependent on the confidence of the golfer to drive between the fairway bunkers. The ideal line is directly between the left and right drive bunkers, shown clearly in the photograph.

The drive bunkers are quite deep (the faces are 8 feet high) and, in most cases, a recovery shot to the green cannot be made. The bunker on the left is 45 yards long and features a small heather covered island. The carry to the fairway is 173 yards from the championship tee and the safe landing area is 52 yards wide short

of the bunkers. The fairway narrows 27 yards between the drive bunkers. The golfer has to decide whether to lay up short of the bunkers on the right leaving a long and tricky shot to the green, or to thread a long straight drive leaving an easier approach shot. The fairway tends to slope to the right.

Bunker at 222 yards

Bunker at 242 yards

VIEW FROM THE 2ND TEE

Green Complex

The Second Shot

From the centre of the fairway, the length of the second shot is obviously determined by the club selection from the tee. The main hazards are the long bunker leading up to the front of the green on the left and the cavernous bunker on the front right. Other than light rough, there are no hazards at the back of the green. The ground dips just short of the green which tends to make the flag look closer than it actually is. The ground also tends to slope to the right.

The Green

The green is 27 yards long and has a slight dip running through the middle. The borrows can be fairly pronounced depending on the flag position.

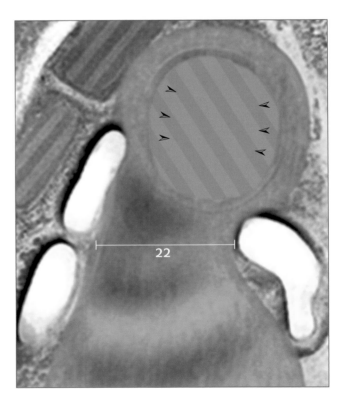

THE HOTCHKIN COURSE – WOODHALL SPA

HOLE 3

| Championship Tee | Medal Tee | Yellow Tee | Ladies Tee |

A medium length, slight dog-leg right, par 4 hole. This is the only hole on the course where the tee shot is blind due to a large bank some 100 yards in front of the tee.

O.B.

28

57

88 MOUND

113

130

149 TREE LEFT

178 SILVER BIRCH

289

266

target area from tee

41

29

0

The Tee Shot (driver)

Like the first and second hole, the prevailing wind is normally behind. The ideal line is a little to the right of the path on the bank, shown clearly in the photograph.

The carry to the fairway is 130 yards and the landing area is 32 yards wide. The first drive bunker is at 289 yards from the championship tee. This bunker is normally only reached when the ground is firm.

Bunker at
289 yards

VIEW FROM THE 3RD TEE

The Second Shot

From the centre of the fairway the length of the second shot is about 160 – 170 yards from the ideal landing area. Once again, the trouble is at the front of the green, with bunkers left and right. There are two bunkers on the left and one small pot bunker on the right.

The Green

The green is 28 yards long and is predominantly flat.

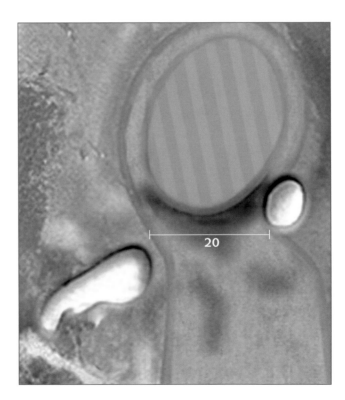

THE HOTCHKIN COURSE – WOODHALL SPA

HOLE 4

A classic heathland dog-leg (left) par 4 of medium length with cavernous bunkers protecting the green.

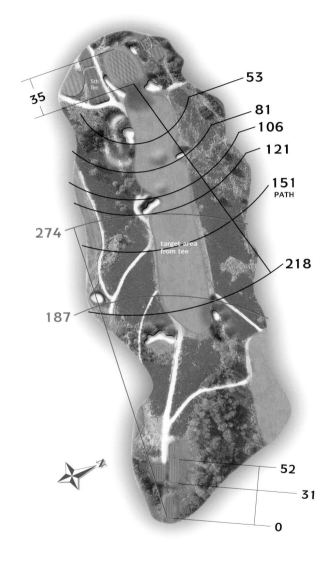

Championship Tee

Medal Tee

Yellow Tee

Ladies Tee

The Tee Shot (firm conditions – fairway wood/long iron, damp conditions – driver)

From the tee the fairway appears quite narrow but is actually 29 yards wide. The ideal line from the championship tee is shown in the photograph.

Generally played into the prevailing wind, club selection is vitally important. The carry to the fairway is 164 yards from the championship tee and, other than the heather bordering both sides of the fairway, the main hazard is the bunker on the left hand side. From the championship tee, this bunker is 274 yards but can be reached when the ground is firm. From the forward tees, the bunker can be as little as 220 yards away and is waiting to gather any drive hit down the left hand side. The fairway also slopes slightly downhill in the landing area.

Bunker at 274 yards

VIEW FROM THE 4TH TEE

Green Complex

The Second Shot

The ideal tee shot leaves a second shot of approximately 150 yards into an elevated green. The bunker on the left hand side of the green is very deep, the lip being some 11 feet high. The bunker on the front right is shallower and the lip is more angled. There is another bunker on the back right hand side of the green that can gather a ball that is struck too firmly into the green.

The Green

The green is 35 yards long (second longest on the course) and slopes gently from left to right. There is a steep slope at the front of the green.

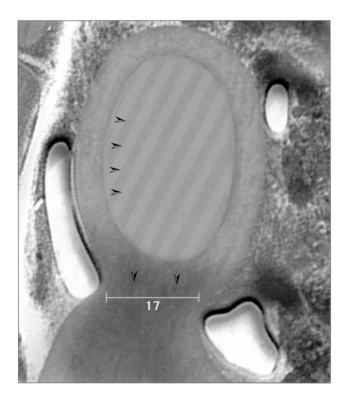

17

THE HOTCHKIN COURSE – WOODHALL SPA

HOLE 5

From the championship tee this hole measures 148 yards and 143 yards from the yellow tee. The prevailing wind is against the golfer and the target is a narrow green some 38 yards long. Deep bunkers surround the green on both sides. There is a small raised ledge at the front of the green measuring about 4 yards and the remainder of the green is predominantly flat.

Green Complex

Championship Tee

Medal Tee

Yellow Tee

Ladies Tee

Courtesy of C Reiners

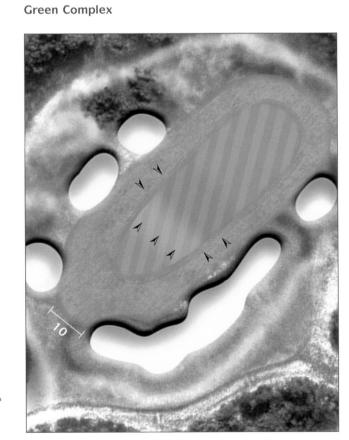

THE HOTCHKIN COURSE – WOODHALL SPA

HOLE 6

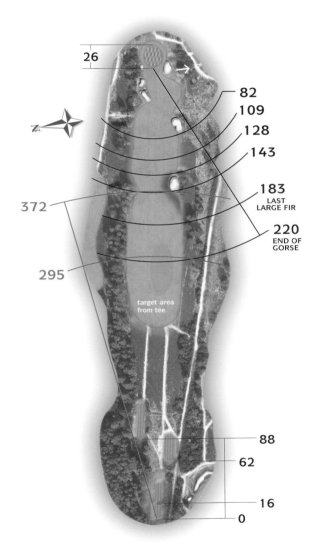

26

82
109
128
143

183
LAST
LARGE FIR

220
END OF
GORSE

372

295

target area
from tee

88
62

16
0

HOTCHKIN COURSE
6
526 YDS
—481 MTRS—
PAR   S.I.
5   ●   1
WOODHALL SPA

Championship Tee

HOTCHKIN COURSE
6
510 YDS
—466 MTRS—
PAR   S.I.
5   ○   1
WOODHALL SPA

Medal Tee

HOTCHKIN COURSE
6
464 YDS
—424 MTRS—
PAR   S.I.
4   ●   1
WOODHALL SPA

Yellow Tee

HOTCHKIN COURSE
6
410 YDS
—374 MTRS—
PAR   S.I.
5   ●   1
WOODHALL SPA

Ladies Tee

From the championship and medal tees this hole plays as a par 5 but as a par 4 from the general play tee. The hole is straight with strategic bunkering close to the green.

The Tee Shot (driver)

From the championship tee, the carry over the heather to the fairway is 219 yards and the ideal line is shown in the photograph. From the general play tee, the carry reduces to 157 yards and, although the fairway is quite generous (33 yards wide), a slope in the ideal landing area tends to cause the ball to bounce to the left. The prevailing wind is behind and the ideal line is indicated. There are no bunkers in range from the tee.

VIEW FROM THE 6TH TEE

The Second Shot

From the centre of the fairway, the golfer is faced with another strategic decision to make. Two well placed pot bunkers some thirty yards short of the green protect the left hand side and the ground slopes a little towards them. To hit the green in two, these bunkers and one on the front right must be negotiated. When laying up, club selection is vital. The bunkers on the left also tend to foreshorten the hole.

The Green

The green is 26 yards long and gently slopes from right to left. Gorse bushes are close to the left hand side of the green.

Green Complex

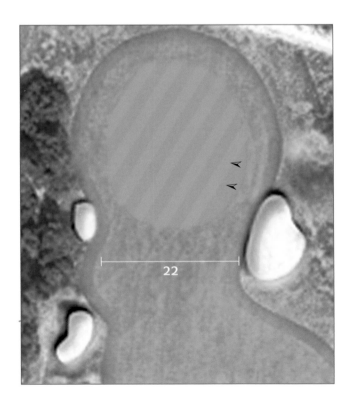

THE HOTCHKIN COURSE – WOODHALL SPA

HOLE 7

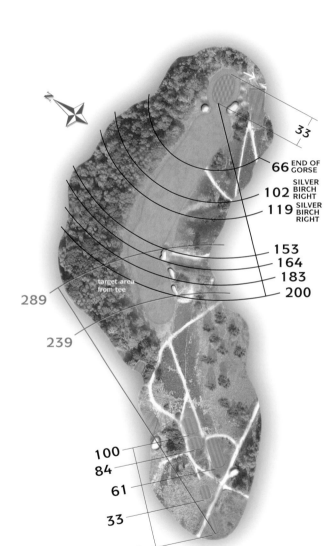

Championship Tee   Medal Tee   Yellow Tee   Ladies Tee

A long dog-leg right par 4 with right hand drive bunkers on the dog-leg.

33

66 END OF GORSE

102 SILVER BIRCH RIGHT

119 SILVER BIRCH RIGHT

153
164
183
200

289

239

target area from tee

100
84
61
33
0

The Tee Shot (driver)

From the championship tee the carry over the heather to the fairway is 220 yards reducing to 150 yards from the general play tee. The prevailing wind is normally helping from the left and the safe line is shown on the photograph.

There are three drive bunkers on the right hand side (which are in range from the various tees). It is possible that these bunkers can be carried but is clearly dependent on the golfer's ability and weather conditions. There is more room on the left hand side of the fairway than it appears, particularly from the championship and medal tees. The fairway is 29 yards wide in the landing area and the rough on the left can be quite severe.

Last Bunker at
289 yards

First Bunker at
239 yards

VIEW FROM THE 7TH TEE

The Second Shot

From the ideal landing area, a second shot between 160 - 180 yards remains. There are two bunkers at the front of the green and gorse bushes protect the left hand side. The ground is slightly raised in front of the green making the second shot tricky to judge.

The Green

The green is 33 yards long and gently slopes from right to left.

Green Complex

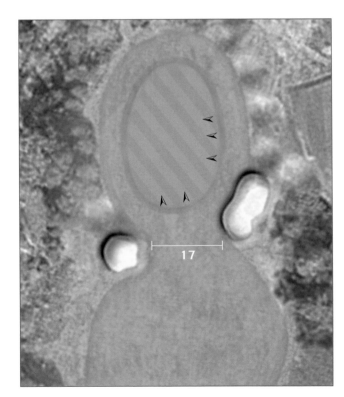

THE HOTCHKIN COURSE – WOODHALL SPA

Championship Tee   Medal Tee   Yellow Tee   Ladies Tee

HOLE 8

From the championship tee this hole measures 209 yards and 187 yards from the yellow tee. The prevailing wind is against the golfer and the target is a large green some 31 yards long. Deep bunkers protect the green at the front on both sides. There is a slope at the front and on the right hand side of the green and a ball landing short right is almost certain to finish in the bunker. The green is kidney shaped and a ball struck too strongly on the left hand side will bounce over the humps and into the heather.

Green Complex

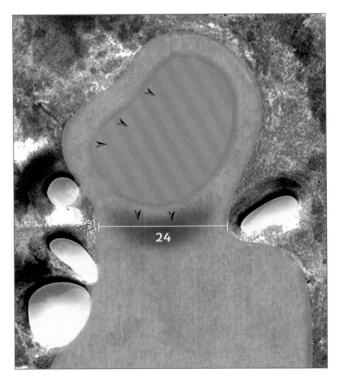

THE HOTCHKIN COURSE – WOODHALL SPA

HOLE 9

The longest hole on the course, this par 5 measures 584 yards from the Championship tee. The hole plays straight with notable cross bunkers.

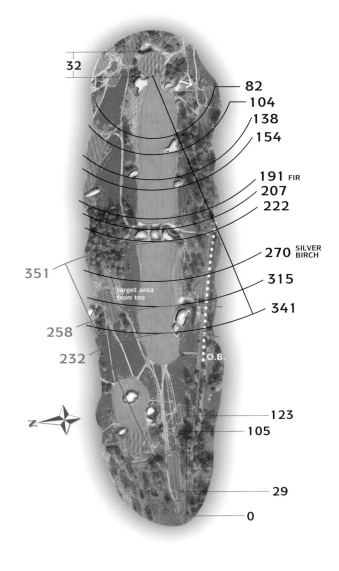

32
82
104
138
154
191 FIR
207
222
270 SILVER BIRCH
315
341
351
target area from tee
258
232
O.B.
123
105
29
0

N

Championship Tee

Medal Tee

Yellow Tee

Ladies Tee

The Tee Shot (driver)

From the championship tee, the carry over the heather to the fairway is 188 yards. From the general play tee, the carry reduces to 150 yards and although the fairway is quite generous (33 yards wide), two deep drive bunkers on the right are in play. The prevailing wind is behind and the ideal line is shown on the photograph. The fairway slopes from right to left in the landing area.

Last Bunker at 232 yards

VIEW FROM THE 9TH TEE

The Second Shot

From the centre of the fairway, the second shot requires a straight hit to a narrowing fairway near the green. There are two deep fairway bunkers on the right and one on the left, sited in a staggered formation. The green is protected by a large bunker on the left and a pot bunker on the right. Gorse also comes into play by the green. Choice of club is dependent on the golfer's intentions and abilities but the aim is to stay in play.

The Green

The green is 32 yards long and apart from a severe bank on the front right, it is predominantly flat.

Green Complex

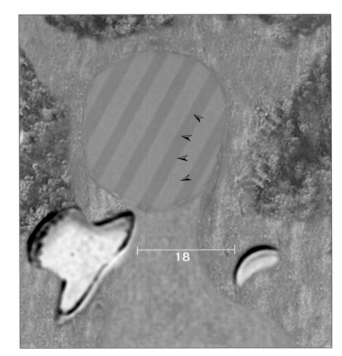

THE HOTCHKIN COURSE – WOODHALL SPA

HOLE 10

A short dog-leg par 4 measuring 338 yards from the championship tee, this hole is a classic example of how a hole does not need to be long to be difficult. The architect's intention was for the golfer to lay up short of the right hand drive bunker and then face a second shot of about 100 yards to a difficult green. Played from a tee surrounded by pine and birch trees, this hole reaches the extremities of the course with the green being the furthest point from the clubhouse.

Championship Tee

Medal Tee

Yellow Tee

Ladies Tee

The Tee Shot (long iron or fairway wood)

An accurate tee shot is required to avoid the deep fairway bunkers. Club selection from the tee depends on the weather and ground conditions; the prevailing wind is normally behind. The carry to the fairway from the championship tee is 188 yards. The drive bunker on the left is at 228 yards and the one on the right is at 269 yards. It is difficult to hit the green from either of these bunkers and when the course is firm, they can be easily reached. The fairway slopes from right to left so the ideal line is to aim a little to the right and allow the bounce to take the ball into the middle of the fairway. The ideal landing area is 28 yards wide. The fairway narrows to 21 yards around the dog-leg.

Last Bunker at 228 yards   Last Bunker at 252 yards

VIEW FROM THE 10TH TEE

The Second Shot

The second shot is normally in the region of 90 - 100 yards and can be extremely difficult to judge. The architect has made excellent use of the slight rise in the ground just short of the green, making the flag appear closer than it actually is.

The Green

The green is slightly elevated and there is a shelf (measuring 10 yards) at the front. After the shelf the green dips to the back. The green is 31 yards long with more pronounced borrows.

Green Complex

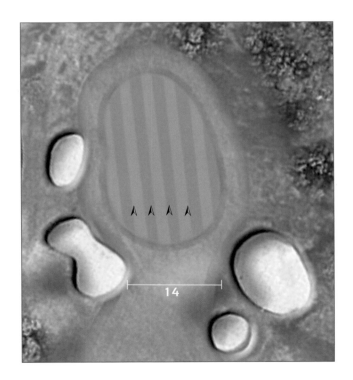

THE HOTCHKIN COURSE – WOODHALL SPA

HOLE 11

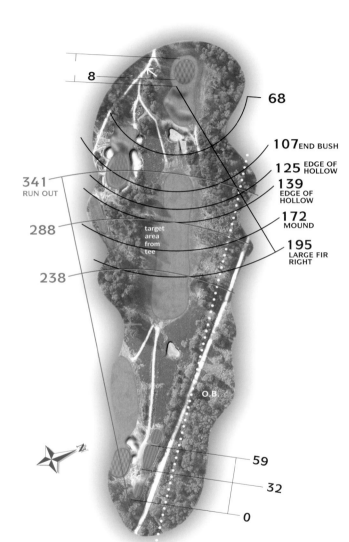

8

68

107END BUSH

125 EDGE OF HOLLOW

139 EDGE OF HOLLOW

172 MOUND

195 LARGE FIR RIGHT

341 RUN OUT

288

target area from tee

238

O.B.

59

32

0

Championship Tee

Medal Tee

Yellow Tee

Ladies Tee

This is one of the most photographed holes on the course with spectacular views from the tee. From the championship tee the hole measures 437 yards and is timeless in design and appearance.

The Tee Shot (driver)

From the championship tee, a carry of 180 yards over heather is required before the fairway is reached, reducing to 150 yards from the general play tee. There is a bunker short of the fairway and in the heather but this only comes into play when the drive is mishit. The prevailing wind is left to right and the ideal line is shown in the photograph. The fairway is relatively flat in the landing area but narrows the further the tee shot is struck. Heavy rough exists on either side of the fairway.

VIEW FROM THE 11TH TEE

The Second Shot

The second shot is very deceiving and it easy to hit one club less than is actually needed. Once again, the architect has achieved 'dead ground' as the flag always looks closer than it actually is. Another factor that needs to be borne in mind is the unusual effect of the wind. It tends to funnel against the backdrop of tall trees surrounding the green and can have the effect of 'knocking the ball down'.

The length of the second shot can vary dramatically depending on the conditions but typically could be in the region of 170 yards. Cross bunkers feature 68 yards short of the green and thick wiry rough extends the length of the green on the left. There is a bank at the front of the green that is more severe than it looks from the fairway.

The Green

The green measures 27 yards and is predominantly flat once over the bank on the front of the green. The bank itself is 8 yards long.

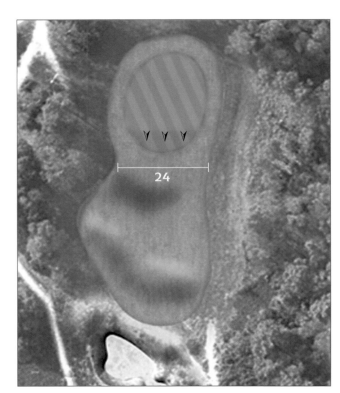

THE HOTCHKIN COURSE – WOODHALL SPA

HOLE 12

Championship Tee

Medal Tee

Yellow Tee

Ladies Tee

The last of three great par 3's, this exceptional hole has featured in golf magazines all over the world. This hole is played through the trees to a slightly elevated green against a backdrop of magnificent pines, birches and gorse. Some of the deepest bunkers on the course (with faces in excess of 11 feet) surround this green.

Green Complex

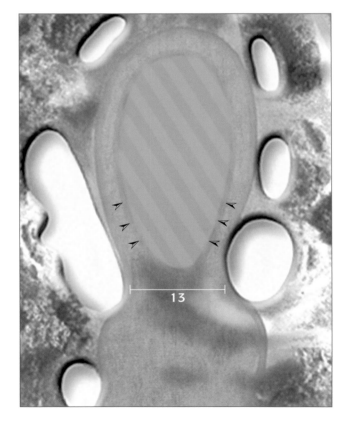

THE HOTCHKIN COURSE – WOODHALL SPA

HOLE 13

One of the toughest par 4's on the course, this hole is played into the prevailing wind, winding through the heather and trees with little room for error. The hole is a slight dog-leg to the right and requires two precise hits to reach the green safely. From the championship tee the hole measures 451 yards and 428 yards from the yellow tee.

Championship Tee

Medal Tee

Yellow Tee

Ladies Tee

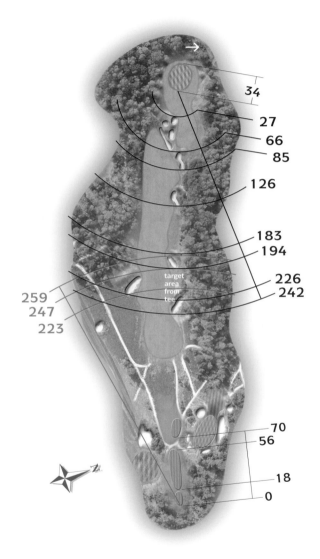

34

27

66

85

126

183

194

target
area
from
tee

226

242

259
247
223

70

56

18

0

The Tee Shot (driver)

The line from the tee is just inside the drive bunker on the left. The carry to the fairway from the championship tee is 150 yards and the fairway slopes slightly to the right in the landing area. The two drive bunkers on the right are 207 and 247 yards respectively and the one on the left is at 223 yards. The ground tends to gather the ball into the bunkers on the right. The fairway is 25 yards wide in the landing area. Heather abounds the fairway both left and right short of the bunkers.

Bunker at 223 yards

Bunker at 247 yards

VIEW FROM THE 13TH TEE

The Second Shot

From the centre of the fairway, the second shot is very dependent on the wind. A long iron shot is invariably required and when the wind is strong, the group of bunkers some 60 yards short of the green can be intimidating to golfers of all levels. The rough running down the left side of the hole from the bunker to the green is very thick. Any shot that lands a fraction short and on line for the right half of the green tends to kick to the right and the rough in this area is very thick.

The Green

The green is 34 yards long and predominantly flat with a little rise to a shelf at the back. The borrows are slight but clear.

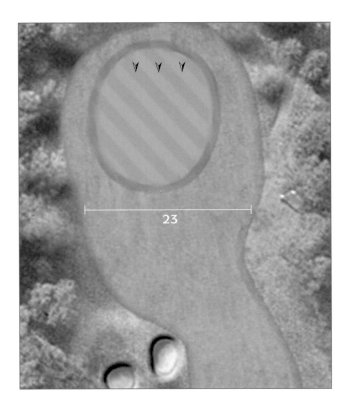

THE HOTCHKIN COURSE – WOODHALL SPA

HOLE 14

| Championship Tee | Medal Tee | Yellow Tee | Ladies Tee |

14 521 YDS —476 MTRS— PAR S.I. 5 8

14 488 YDS —446 MTRS— PAR S.I. 5 8

14 457 YDS —418 MTRS— PAR S.I. 5 8

14 276 YDS —252 MTRS— PAR S.I. 5 8

A slight dog-leg par 5 measuring 521 yards from championship tee and 457 yards from the general play tee (still played as a par 5) is normally played into the prevailing wind. The key to playing this hole well is knowing the line off the tee and making the right decision to either attempt to hit the green in two, or to lay up short of the bunker some 40 yards from the green.

28

50

108
END TREES
LEFT

176 SILVER
BIRCH
COPSE

target
area 2
from tee

236
MOUND

272

297

target
area 1
from tee

257
MOUND

230

204
MOUND

O.B.

98

75 64

33

0

The Tee Shot (driver)

There are five tees on this hole and the ideal line to the fairway is dependent on the golfer's ability. Shorter hitters need to keep left, whereas the longer hitters should aim over the staggered bunkers on the right (see graphic on page 119). From the championship tee, the ideal line is between the second and third bunkers. From the medal and yellow tees, the bunkers can be flown and the line is typically over the third bunker depending on the golfer's ability. Once again, a shot to the left is quite safe. The fairway is 30 yards wide. When the conditions are firm, this fairway is particularly fast running and long hitters need to be aware of the ball running through the dog-leg.

Third Bunker at
204 yards

Last Bunker
257 yards carry

VIEW FROM THE 14TH TEE

The Second Shot

From the middle of the fairway the golfer faces a narrow target as he looks down the hole. Trees, gorse and heather line the fairway on both sides but the most threatening hazard is the bunker some 50 yards short of the green on the left. This bunker needs to be negotiated at some point and if it is considered that the carry is too long, a lay up shot is the most sensible. The ground dips and slopes to the right in front of the green.

The Green

The green is 28 yards long surrounded by a bank. There is a small pot bunker on the front right of the green and a ditch runs some ten yards right and to the back of the green. The green is predominantly flat.

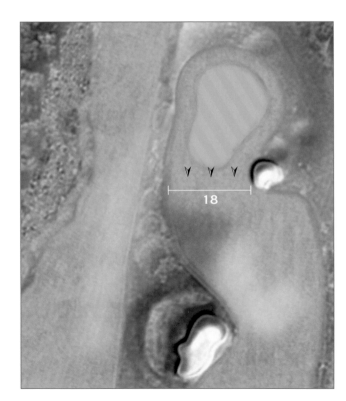

THE HOTCHKIN COURSE – WOODHALL SPA

HOLE 15

29
35
276
101
123
139
END TREE LEFT
206
185

target area from tee

40

0

Championship Tee   Medal Tee   Yellow Tee   Ladies Tee

A tricky short par 4 that requires a well positioned tee shot. Another example of a hole that does not need to be long to be difficult.

The Tee Shot (iron)

There is only one tee on this hole and there is little difference between the various lengths. It is the only hole on the course where the fairway is elevated from the tee. This hole has been designed with the intention of the golfer laying up of the drive bunkers on the right (185 yards to the first one). The ideal line is just to the left of these bunkers as shown in the photograph. The landing area is 39 yards and the wind is normally right to left.

It is not difficult to fly these bunkers (carry 209 yards) but the fairway is extremely narrow and the penalty for missing the fairway is severe. Heather, gorse and trees line both sides of the fairway.

Bunker
206 yards carry

VIEW FROM THE 15TH TEE

The Second Shot

When playing from the ideal landing area, a shot of about 130 yards is required. Bunkers surround the green.

The Green

The green is 29 yards long and is in a basin.

Green Complex

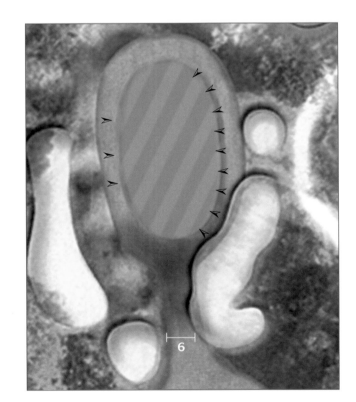

THE HOTCHKIN COURSE – WOODHALL SPA

HOLE 16

| Championship Tee | Medal Tee | Yellow Tee | Ladies Tee |

16 395 YDS — 361 MTRS — PAR 4 S.I. 4

16 395 YDS — 361 MTRS — PAR 4 S.I. 4

16 367 YDS — 335 MTRS — PAR 4 S.I. 4

16 318 YDS — 291 MTRS — PAR 4 S.I. 4

A medium length short par 4 with a deceptively long carry to the fairway.

29

47

335

110 FIR

123 MOUND

274
LARGE FIR

target
area
from
tee

160
END TREE
LEFT

70

28

0

The Tee Shot (wind dependent)

From the championship tee this hole measures 395 yards. The carry to the fairway is 195 yards, reducing to 125 yards from the yellow tee. Normally played into the prevailing wind, the choice of club is dependent on the conditions. The ideal line (shown in the photograph) is to finish on the right half of the fairway. The trees on the right are close to the fairway and the rough on the left can be very lush.

VIEW FROM THE 16TH TEE

THE HOTCHKIN COURSE – WOODHALL SPA

The Second Shot

When playing from the ideal landing area, a shot of about 130 yards is required. There are no bunkers around the green, the only one on the hole being 47 yards short of the front edge.

The Green

The green is 29 yards long and is predominantly flat. There is slight dip running across the middle of the green.

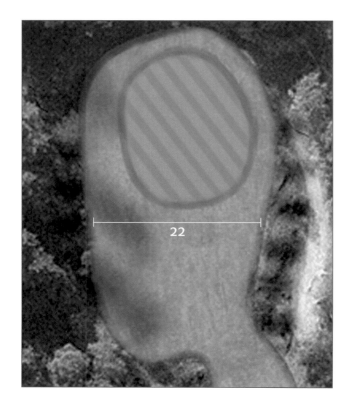

THE HOTCHKIN COURSE – WOODHALL SPA

HOLE 17

Championship Tee

Medal Tee

Yellow Tee

Ladies Tee

A short dog-leg left par 4 requiring a strategic tee shot followed by an accurate second shot. Even though the hole may look simple, the architect has questioned the golfer's ability to play strategically and safely to a difficult green.

66 SILVER BIRCH

80 SILVER BIRCH

109

144 SILVER BIRCH

target area 2 from tee

target area 1 from tee

31

262

220

45

0

The Tee Shot (long iron or fairway wood)

Like the 15th hole, there is little difference in length between the various tees. From the championship tee, this hole measures 336 yards and the carry to the fairway is 165 yards, reducing to 151 yards from the yellow tee. Mounds also feature just short of the fairway that restricts the view of the left hand side of the hole. Normally played into the prevailing wind, the choice of club is dependent on the conditions. A strategic decision has to be made on the club selection. A right hand drive pot bunker placed at 220 yards poses the biggest threat from the tee. Choosing a club that leaves the tee shot short of this hazard is wise, particularly as the fairway is 45 yards wide at this point. A more aggressive approach is to drive the ball past the bunker into a narrow fairway (25 yards wide) leaving a short pitch to the green. The rough can be quite penal on the left hand side. Taking the safer option, the ideal line (shown in the photograph) is to be in the right half of the fairway. The trees on the right past the bunker are close to the fairway and a tee shot can easily run into them because of the camber of the fairway at this point.

Bunker at 220 yards

VIEW FROM THE 17TH TEE

The Second Shot

When playing from the safe option area, a shot of about 120 yards is required. If a stronger tee shot is played past the bunker a relatively short pitch is required. There are six deep bunkers around the green.

The Green

The green is 31 yards long and slopes from left to right. The borrows are quite obvious.

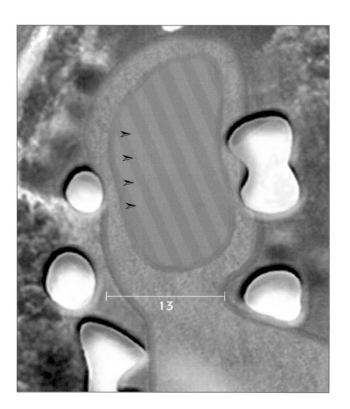

THE HOTCHKIN COURSE – WOODHALL SPA

HOLE 18

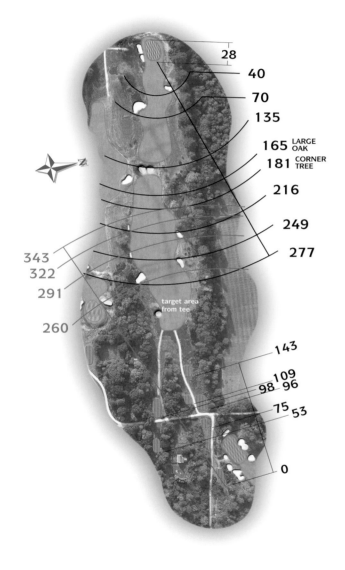

28
40
70
135
165 LARGE OAK
181 CORNER TREE
216
249
277
343
322
291
260
target area from tee
143
109
98 96
75 53
0

Championship Tee

Medal Tee

Yellow Tee

Ladies Tee

This strong finishing hole dog-legs slightly from left to right and plays as a par 5 from the championship tee. From the yellow tee, the hole is played as a long par 4.

The Tee Shot (driver)

From the championship tee, this hole measures 540 yards. The carry to the fairway is 200 yards and when played into the prevailing wind, the tee shot is very demanding. The ideal line is in the middle or slightly left. Any shot to the right is blocked out by a large oak tree near the dog-leg.

From the yellow tee, the carry to the fairway is very much reduced (102 yards) although a similar line is required. The large oak tree is more in play from this tee and a tee shot favouring the left hand side is desirable. There are two drive bunkers on the right hand side and four on the left. It is not possible to gain much distance out of these bunkers. The fairway is generous (44 yards) and flat.

VIEW FROM THE 18TH TEE

The Second Shot

When playing from the ideal landing area, a long second shot is required to hit the green in two. As well as the large oak on the dog-leg, there are cross bunkers located at 135 yards from the green. There are two bunkers (one on the left and one on the right) situated between 70 and 40 yards which present a real hazard when laying up. There are two bunkers on the left hand side of the green. A ball landing just short and right of the green tends to kick favourably to the left although one landing green high will bounce straight or even a little right.

The Green

The green is 28 yards long and is slightly raised at the front. The remainder of the green is reasonably flat but there are some gentle borrows in places.

Green Complex

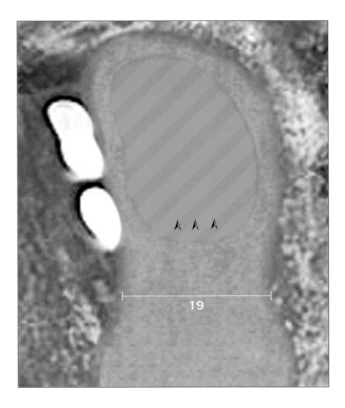

THE HOTCHKIN COURSE – WOODHALL SPA

Over the past 100 years there have been many exciting rounds of golf played, tremendous team performances, and championships won and lost on the 18th hole. A complete list of national and international events played is given in Chapter 7. Many local and regional tournaments have also been played on The Hotchkin course and the very popular Central England Foursomes Events are played on an annual basis. It is not the remit of this book to discuss these events but it is considered that the story would not be complete without mentioning the course records:

1. During an exhibition match in 1946 Bobby Locke achieved a round of 69 (course length 6,805 yards).

2. Bill Wood's excellent course record of 66 was achieved during the Lincolnshire Amateur Championship in 1973 (course length 6,823 yards).

3. Raife Hutt scored 68 in the British Youths Championship in 1991 (course length 6,970 yards). Dean Robertson equalled his score the following day.

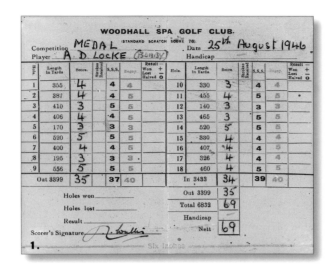

1.

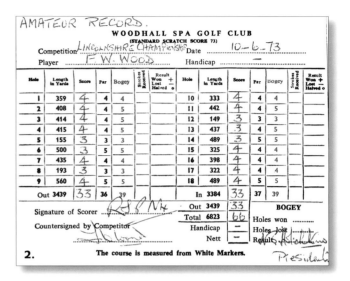

2.

3.

ENGLISH GOLF UNION
THE ENGLISH COUNTY CHAMPIONS TOURNAMENT FOR THE PRESIDENTS BOWL 1998

S.S.S.75

Name _____ Gary Wolstenholme

Hole	1	2	3	4	5	6	7	8	9	Out
Yards	361	442	415	414	148	510	470	192	584	3536
Par	4	4	4	4	3	5	4	3	5	36
Score	4	4	3	4	2	4	4	3	4	32

Playing Handicap _____ +2 _____ Date _____ 19.9.1998

Hole	10	11	12	13	14	15	16	17	18	In	Total
Yards	338	437	172	451	521	321	395	336	540	3511	7047
Par	4	4	3	4	5	4	4	4	5	37	73
Score	3	4	3	4	5	3	5	4	4	35	67

4. Signature of Competitor _____

Signature of Marker _____

4. Gary Wolstenholme scored 67 in the County Champions of Champions Tournament in 1998 (course length 7,047 yards)

5. When the course was lengthened to 7,080 yards, Jochen Lupprian from Germany scored 68 on route to winning the Brabazon Trophy in 2000. James Crampton broke this record by one shot, scoring 67 in the Midland Open in 2004. Paul Thomason then beat this record in 2004 with an outstanding round of 66 in the Midland Qualifying for the EGU County Championships (course length 7,080 yards).

6. The ladies course record is held by Anne Thompson with an excellent round of 69. This score was recorded in 1987 and has yet to be beaten. Scores lower than 69 have been recorded in national ladies events, but the course used for these events was a composite course between the men's and ladies' tees.

PLEASE AVOID SLOW PLAY AT ALL TIMES

COMPETITION Midland Qualifier for EGU County Champs — DATE 19/6/2004 — TIME 15.17pm

Player A — P Thomason — Handicap 1 — Strokes Received

Player B — Leicester & Rutland — Handicap — Strokes Received

Marker's Score	Hole	CHAMP Yards	MEDAL Yards	Par	YELLOW Yards	Par	Stroke Index	GROSS SCORE A	B	Nett Score	Points	RED Yards	Par	Stroke Index
	1	361	361	4	353	4	17	4				327	4	17
	2	442	411	4	401	4	7	3				351	4	7
	3	415	415	4	408	4	3	3				370	4	3
	4	414	414	4	383	4	11	4				358	4	11
	5	148	148	3	143	3	16	3				113	3	16
	6	526	510	5	464	4	1	3				410	5	1
	7	470	437	4	409	4	9	4				366	4	9
	8	209	192	3	187	3	13	3				164	3	13
	9	584	555	5	545	5	5	5				459	5	5
	OUT	3569	3443	36	3293	35		32				2918	36	
	10	338	338	4	328	4	12	3				276	4	12
	11	437	437	4	405	4	6	4				372	4	6
	12	172	172	3	144	3	18	3				123	3	18
	13	451	451	4	428	4	2	5				381	4	2
	14	521	488	5	457	5	8	4				420	5	8
	15	321	321	4	315	4	14	3				289	4	14
	16	395	395	4	367	4	4	4				318	4	4
	17	336	336	4	322	4	15	4				280	4	15
	18	540	540	5	442	4	10	4				395	5	10
	IN	3511	3478	37	3208	36		34				2854	37	
	OUT	3569	3443	36	3293	35		32				2918	36	
	TOT	7080	6921	73	6501	71		66				5772	73	

Stableford points or par result

HANDICAP 1

NETT SCORE 65

PLEASE INDICATE TEE USED SSS 75 SSS 73 SSS 74

5. Marker's Signature _____ T. McJanet. — Player's Signature _____

LADIES' AMATEUR RECORD

L.G.U. STANDARD SCRATCH SCORE 74
(Handicaps calculated against S.S.S. NOT Par)

Woodhall Spa Golf Club — Ladies' Scoring Card

Competition CAPTAIN'S DAY — Date 2/7/87

Player ANNE THOMPSON — Handicap SCRATCH

Marker's Score	Hole	Yards	Metres	Score	Stroke Index	Par	Bogey	Result Won Lost Halved	Marker's Score	Hole	Yards	Metres	Score	Stroke Index	Par	Bogey	Result Won Lost Halved
	1	321	293	4	7	4	4			10	279	255	4	12	4	4	
	2	357	326	4	17	4	5			11	376	344	4	6	4	5	
	3	371	339	4	3	4	5			12	116	106	3	16	3	3	
	4	353	322	4	13	4	5			13	381	349	4	2	4	5	
	5	113	103	3	15	3	3			14	419	384	4	10	5	5	
	6	412	377	4	1	5	5			15	291	266	4	14	4	4	
	7	369	337	3	11	4	4			16	318	291	4	4	4	4	
	8	162	149	3	9	3	3			17	276	252	4	18	4	4	
	9	463	423	5	5	5	5			18	394	361	4	8	5	5	
	Out 2921	2669		34		36	39			In 2850	2608		35		37	39	

Signature of Scorer _____ John M. Pipe.

Countersigned by Competitor _____ A. Thompson.

Out 2921	2669	34
In 2850	2608	35
Total 5771	5277	69
Handicap		
Nett		

Bogey Result

Stableford

Points out

Points in

TOTAL

6.

CHAPTER 7 ~ MAJOR EVENTS

The first national event to be played at Woodhall Spa was the English Ladies' Championship in 1926. This event was a great success and certainly brought the course to the attention of the golfing world. Alterations to the course continued well into the 1930s and newspaper reports throughout this period continued to highlight the course as an ideal tournament venue.

The English Golf Union first used the course in the mid 1930s for a trial match. The war put an end to golf events during the 1940s. From the 1950s onwards, Woodhall Spa was then considered as a regular tournament venue and has hosted most of the major amateur events. The desire to hold professional events never existed and although approached on several occasions, the Hotchkin family chose not to participate. A list of the events played to date is given opposite:

Key to the events:

The Brabazon Trophy (inaugurated in 1957) is the English Open Amateur Stroke Play Championship and is regarded as one of the leading amateur stroke play events in Europe.

The English Amateur Championship is a match play event for male golfers affiliated to English golf clubs.

The Home Internationals is where the four home nations play against one another in a three day event.

The Vagliano Trophy - Biennial match for teams of women representing GB&I and Europe.

The St Andrews Trophy - Biennial match for teams of men representing GB&I and Europe.

Date	Event	Result
1926	The English Ladies' Close Championship	M Gourlay
1953	The British Girls' Open Amateur Championship	S Hill bt A Ward 3/2
1954	The English Ladies' Close Championship	F Stephens bt E Price
	The Brabazon Trophy	P F Scrutton (302)
	The English Counties Championship	Cheshire
1962	The English Ladies' Close Amateur Championship	J Roberts bt A Bonallack 3/1
	The Brabazon Trophy	A Slater (290) bt A E Shepperson (290) in 18 hole play off
1966	The Ladies' Home Internationals	England
1967	The English Amateur Championship	M F Bonallack bt G E Hyde 4/2
1972	The English Ladies' Close Amateur Championship	M Everard bt A Bonallack
1972	The English Counties Championship	BB&O
1974	The English Amateur Championship	M James bt J A Watts 6/5
1976	Oxford v Cambridge University Golf Match	Cambridge
1978	The Brabazon Trophy	G Brand Jr (289)
1979	The British Youths Championship	G Brand Jr (291)
	GB & I v Continent of Europe (youths)	GB&I 12 Europe 3
1980	Ladies' British Open Amateur Championship	A Quast (US) bt L Wollin (Swe) 3/1
1981	The Men's Home Internationals Championship	Scotland
1983	The Vagliano Trophy	GB&I 14 - 10
1984	The English Amateur Championship	D Gilford bt M Gerrard 4/3
1990	The English Amateur Championship	I D Garbutt bt G Evans 8/7
	The British Youths Championship	J Payne (287)
1994	Ladies' British Open Amateur Stroke Play Championship	K Speak (297)
1995	The European Boys Team Championship	England
1996	The St Andrews Trophy	GB&I 16 - 8
1996	The English Counties Championship	Hants, IW & CI
	GB&I v Continent of Europe (Jacques Leglise Trophy)	Europe 13 - 11
1998	The English Amateur Championship	M Sanders bt S Gorry 6/5
2000	The Brabazon Trophy	J Lupprian (68, 72, 72,72 = 284)
2001	The Men's Home International Championship	England
2002	The British Seniors' Open Amateur Championship	J Baldwin (216)
2004	The English Ladies' Close Strokeplay Championship	S Reddick (69, 69, 71, 76 = 286)

Harry Vardon (1870 - 1937)

Harry Vardon was born on May 9th 1870 in Grouville on the island of Jersey. He was one of eight children (six boys and two girls) and had a modest upbringing. He and his family became familiar with golf when the game was introduced on the island near to his home. Because the land was so natural, the course was laid out by mainly marking areas for tees and greens and golf started shortly afterwards. The course later became Royal Jersey Golf Club and Vardon, along with his two brothers Tom and Fred, became enthusiastic about the game through their caddying activities. It is reported that they made their own clubs from scraps of wood, carefully carving shafts from branches and shaping heads from memory of the real clubs they had seen whilst caddying. Interestingly, they secured the heads to the shaft by boring a hole through the head using a red hot poker. This was quite ingenious for young lads and it was a few years before club makers introduced the technique of securing heads to shafts. Both his brothers, Tom and Fred, became club professionals at notable clubs. In particular, Tom was appointed the professional at Royal St George's and was also a fine player.

Harry Vardon's first appointment as a professional was at Ripon Golf Club but he moved soon afterwards to a busier club at Bury. He started to compete by playing in exhibition matches and professional tournaments and became good friends with J H Taylor. He played in his first Open Championship at Prestwick in 1893. In 1894, his game had improved quite dramatically and he finished 5th in the Open at Royal St George's. The following year he was appointed professional at Ganton and then went on to win the Open in 1896 at Muirfield. He was to win the Open six times in all, the last in 1914 when he was 44. He also won the US Open in 1900 and was runner up on two other occasions.

Harry Vardon clearly had an outstanding playing career and lived in an era when top professionals were consulted on all matters pertaining to golf. He laid out many courses and helped to refine others. Iain Cumming, who has been conducting a study on Vardon's courses, suggests that he was involved in the laying out of at least forty nine courses before the First World War. In particular, it would appear that Woodhall Spa was the fourth 18 hole course that Vardon laid out. It is interesting to note that his first 18 hole course was laid out at Grimsby & Cleethorpes, also in Lincolnshire.

Vardon carried on designing courses both during and after the war and his thinking on course architecture was undoubtedly affected by improvements in equipment and the ball. Interestingly, Vardon's course development programmes remained his own and he did not team up with other architects at any point in his life. This was at time when many of the great partnerships were formed.

His philosophy on the laying out of courses, based on various articles and books that he wrote is summarised as follows:

- Thirty - forty acres is the amount of land required for 9 holes, and a minimum of seventy acres required for 18 holes
- Plenty of time should be taken when planning the actual layout. Holes should be staked out allowing unwanted rocks, gorse, etc to be removed
- Shots should be played from the tee sites to the green sites Ideas for hazard placements will be gathered during this exercise
- A 9 hole course should have seven medium or long holes and two short ones
- The situation of short holes depends largely on the land but, ideally holes 3 and 7 are the perfect location
- Short holes should be reached by an iron at all times (which restricts the length to about 160 yards)
- There should be three or four short holes in a full course and to have the fourth hole of 200 yards is sometimes an interesting option. This hole would require a driver and would give the golfer a great sense of achievement if the green was reached
- The remainder of the course should be made of two and three shot holes of between 370 and 530 yards

- Holes of between 230 - 330 yards are not considered good. However holes of between 370 - 380 yards are considered ideal because a solid drive and second shot is required to reach the green in two

- Courses of 6,000 yards plus were considered too long until the rubber cored ball was introduced. After 1906 there was a sudden burst of course lengthening, particularly those courses that measured less than 6,000 yards

- On course routing (obviously dependent on land available) the direction of play is important. Courses that start with the boundary to the left are preferred as they test the golfer's skill at not pulling shots early in the round. Ideally, the first and tenth holes should be located as close together as possible and be close to the clubhouse

- Bunkers and other hazards should be placed to test the scratch golfer (not the high handicap). Cross bunkering is not favoured, but where they have to be placed they should be about 130 - 145 yards from the tee and directly in front of the green. Bunkers should be placed down either side of the hole to catch wayward shots. Hazards should be the last features to be placed on a new layout and the course should be played in a variety of conditions before their final positions decided

- Green locations are dependent on what land is available. Their size is linked to the length of the second shot. Undulating small greens are particularly appealing.

Harry Shapland Colt (1869 -1951)

Harry Shapland Colt first learned to play golf in 1880 on Malvern Common during his school holidays. He attended Monkton Combe public school near Bath and was an excellent all round sportsman. He attended Clare College, Cambridge to study Law and started to play golf more regularly. He played against Oxford in 1889 and led the team in 1890.

John L Low also attended Clare College and Colt became good friends with him. He was introduced to the R&A through Low and played regularly at St Andrews. He won the Jubilee Vase in 1891 and 1893 and reduced his handicap to scratch in 1893.

Encouraged by F G Tait, he even entered one Open Championship. He joined Royal Wimbledon in 1893 and went to Hastings to join a law practice. He married in 1894.

Whilst in Hastings, Colt assisted with the laying out of the course at Rye and was the first Club Captain. He was appointed Honorary Secretary from 1896 to 1899 and was still overseeing tee construction in 1901 when Sunningdale advertised for their first Secretary.

As the years went by, Colt's advice and time were sought after from all areas of the rapidly expanding golf industry. He still competed at the highest amateur level, playing a number of Amateur Championships, R&A Meetings, club matches and one International. He advised Sutton's, the seeds firm and was hired as an agent to Shanks' mowers. By the outbreak of the First World War, he had produced twelve courses and had already made two trips to North America. By this time he had made connections with Dr Alistair MacKenzie, Hugh Alison and Auguste Legouix who eventually became site manager at Swinley Forest. At the outbreak of war, MacKenzie and Alison enlisted, however Colt himself was too old. As there was little work to be found at this time, in 1916 he moved to the other end of Berkshire, where he purchased a fruit farm, employing Legouix as his farm manager. He also found the time to become a JP for West Berkshire, sitting at Wantage.

After the war Colt, Alison and MacKenzie joined forces again and started their quest for new course designs by writing many articles and books. In particular, *'Some Essays on Golf Course Architecture'* became an important publication for many to follow. Alison went off to America and helped to finish off Colt's missing holes at Pine Valley before designing another twenty courses in

America and Canada. MacKenzie also went to America two years later and laid out twenty courses in California alone. At home, Colt was at the peak of his genius. He produced Wentworth, the New Course at Sunningdale, Moor Park (West), as well as County Sligo and le Mer at Le Touquet. Others courses built at this time include Effingham, Tandridge, Ham Manor, Brancepeth Castle, Northamptonshire, Prestbury, Churston and Trevose. Before the war, he designed St George's Hill, Stoke Poges, Copt Heath, Calcot Park and Camberley Heath. There were 50 courses in Britain that Colt either designed or remodelled and 15 more in Europe. His remodelling work included Muirfield, Lytham St Annes, Hoylake, Ganton, Portrush, Porthcawl, Formby and Woodhall Spa.

Colt's relationship with MacKenzie faded towards the end of the 1920s. The final grouping of Colt, Alison and Morrison was formed in 1928 and continued until 1961. The Depression in 1929, the Second World War and the fact that golf was in the doldrums for nearly 20 years after 1945 meant that work was limited. However, courses in the Far East and in Europe were built. Colt had really finished his involvement in golf by 1939. After the war, he wrote to his partners expressing a wish to resign but they implored him to stay on. There was little work around and Alison went to South Africa. Morrison soldiered on alone and Colt died in 1951, thereby bringing an end to this most able golf architectural triumvirate.

Colt's views on course architecture are as follows:

- Two starting points near the clubhouse, two green sites near the clubhouse allowing for four lines of play, if the site permits this. If natural green sites do not exist then they should be artificially constructed

- First hole should be fairly long and easy
- Avoid hugging the boundary on the first hole, if possible
- Strong finishing hole very desirable
- Make use of as many natural features as possible, including natural sites for greens
- Added interest if the ground immediately before the green can be a ravine or hill
- Blind second shots can add variety; this should not always be dismissed
- Ideal courses should be between 6,000 and 6,300 yards long. If land permits, build with a reserve in mind
- Four short holes preferable
- Variety of length on holes where golfers are required to use most clubs in the bag. A hole that can be hit by one long drive (230 - 300 yards) is often an interesting hole. Best type of green for this hole would be a plateau
- Majority of holes between 380 - 450 yards with a few shorter ones around 330 yards
- Variety of teeing grounds essential so that length of the hole can be altered depending on weather conditions
- Longer holes should not be against the prevailing wind
- Alter direction of holes wherever possible to break the monotony of wind direction
- Avoid skirting the boundary on consecutive holes where possible. If this has to be the case then try and route the holes so the boundary tests hooks and slices. Perhaps test the slices out more
- Steep hills should be played diagonally rather than straight up and down

- If there is one dramatic feature, do not sacrifice several holes to make one great hole. The whole layout must be considered to make the most out of it
- Desirable to postpone the placement of some of the bunkers until the course is ready for play. Bunkers then placed after the run of the ball has been observed
- Carries from the tee to be 110 yards maximum
- Optional carries to the fairway are important
- Placement of bunkers vital to test players of all standards
- Some compulsory carries for the second are important
- Size and shape of the putting green should be governed by the type of shot being played
- Hazards should be difficult but not impossible to play from
- Depth of bunkers should be in proportion to the risk.

Stafford Vere Hotchkin (1876 - 1953)

The architect of The Hotchkin course was Colonel Stafford Vere Hotchkin MC, TD, DL. He was born in 1876 and educated at Shrewsbury School. He married in 1906 and became High Sheriff of the County of Rutland in 1912. He was an officer in the 21st Lancers before joining the Leicestershire Yeomanry with whom he served in the Palestine and Mesopotamia campaigns during World War One achieving the rank of Major. After the war, he became an Honorary Colonel of the 60th Field Regiment RATA.

'The Colonel', as he was affectionately known, was also a Member of Parliament for the Horncastle Division of Lincolnshire, a member of Lincolnshire County Council for 30 years and also the Chairman of the Justices of the Peace at Horncastle for many years.

The Hotchkin family owned a considerable amount of land in and around Woodhall Spa and had provided the site for the golf course in 1903 when it became necessary for the Golf Club to find a new venue. A keen golfer, The Colonel played an important part in the opening ceremonies of the new course in 1905 and played an active part in club affairs until the outbreak of war in 1914.

In the early 1920s, with some assistance of another golf course architect, Cecil Key Hutchison, the Colonel set about redesigning the course at Woodhall Spa with the intention of creating a true championship test. The quality and strength of his design is such that it has stood the test of time, having remained largely unaltered since 1935 (the subject of Chapter 3).

The bulk of this work was carried out between 1922 and 1935. On completion of the initial changes to Woodhall Spa, the Colonel set up a company called Ferigna Limited dealing with all aspects of the golf course business including design, construction, maintenance, equipment, turf dressings and seed. It is reported that the Colonel was fascinated by the fact that grass grew vigorously around railway lines and with a friend, Arthur Taylor, who owned a local foundry, devised some revolutionary iron-based fertilisers. The name Ferigna was created from the use of ferrous materials.

In the winter of 1927/8, the Colonel travelled to South Africa to become involved in the remodelling of Durban, Humewood at Port Elizabeth, Transvaal, Mowbray, Cape Province, East London, Maccauvlei and Royal Port Alfred among many others. Woodhall Spa exerted a major influence on his design work and certain features were incorporated into the above venues.

On his return to England in 1928, Cecil Key Hutchison and Sir Guy Colin Campbell joined Ferigna Ltd. Ferigna undertook the design and construction of several courses in the south of England including Ashridge, Warsash, Shoreham, Leeds Castle and West Sussex. It was during the design of West Sussex that disagreements between the three partners started to emerge which led to an eventual split on completion of the project.

The Colonel worked on numerous other golf courses as a consultant in design, construction and maintenance matters. These included Grimsby, Newmarket, Purley Downs, RAF Cranwell, Stoke Rochford, Sutton-on-Sea, Newmarket Links and remodelling works to Royal Worlington and Newmarket.

The Colonel wrote many articles for golf and sports magazines discussing golf course architecture, drainage of sports fields, and general turf care. The editor of the *Club Sportsman* was so impressed by his articles, he published a collection of his contributions in a small pamphlet - *The Principles of Golf Course Architecture*.

The following list provides a summary of his thoughts:

- The golf architect is not always favoured by nature in the matter of soils. The best types are those of a light sandy composition, seaside, common, moor and downland turf, which are not too frequently found inland

- The best results are obtained by making a course conform to the natural surroundings that already exist, so that it will not look artificial and fail to blend with the landscape

- An eye for scenic effects, as well as a sound knowledge of golfing principles, is a necessary qualification for a modern golf architect. The setting of a green in a pretty background and the use of distant views are an important part of the job

- Every golf hole, as far as is possible, should be a picture unto itself, so that the golfer's mind is concentrated on the actual hole he is playing and is not, as occurs on so many courses, forced to take in a few other holes at the same time

- Much can be learned in the art of construction by spending a few hours at the seaside, studying what nature has created.

- Blind holes should be avoided on principle

- Apart from the best seaside links, many most interesting and excellent courses have been produced on commons. In the old days, this was often done at very low cost, thanks to the natural skill and golfing knowledge of many of the exponents of the game in those times. Use was made to the fullest extent of any natural features, both from the point of view of the game, and more often than not, from financial considerations

- Before the rubber cored ball came into use, the costs of construction and maintenance were considerably less than at present. This of course is due to the larger area of ground now required, the additional length of the courses and the extra labour necessary for upkeep. Simplicity in construction, combined with the requisite knowledge of how to use it, is undoubtedly the highest art in producing the best golfing results, and there is much too big a tendency to create artificial greens and features, which are often both a waste of money and a benefit neither to the landscape nor the golfer

- Some of the best holes are up valleys, and the best greens in hollows and on natural plateaus

- Par three holes ideally should be four - two on the even and two on the odd. Length of 135, 155, 175 and 195 yards are ideal

as they suit golfers of all skills

- The remainder of the holes should vary between 330 and 485 yards and two or three par 5's of over 500 yards

- Entrance to the green is very important and should be dependent on the type of ground and length of shot that is required to be played. Normal width is 17 yards and on longer holes the length is 22 to 26 yards. On short holes you would normally expect somewhere between 9 and 15 yards depending on the length

- Bunkers are dependent on the type of ground and terrain, but where possible make a really bold one.

The above comments provide an insight into the Colonel's views on architecture. Clearly a very knowledgeable man, he designed some excellent courses around the world.

Flora

Many of the plants and trees found on The Hotchkin course are typical of lowland heathland in Britain. Large copses of birch and pine now line most of the fairways. This certainly has not always been the case as many of the photographs in this book illustrate. Various pines were planted when the course first opened but the birches have self-seeded. Oak trees feature on some of the holes, most notably on the 18th hole, providing a strong strategic feature whilst both driving and playing the second shot. Gorse and broom, another feature of heathland, grow abundantly on the course. Most fairways are surrounded by two types of heather (Bell and Ling), which come into bloom at different times of the year (June and August respectively).

In order to provide a flora time capsule, a survey of plant life was carried out by the Lincolnshire Naturalist's Union (recorders were Irene Weston, Paul Kirby, Vi Wilkin, Zella Harris and Roger Labbett) in the summer of 2004.

Trees and shrubs

(38 species recorded to date)

Alder	*Alnus glutinosa*
Alder Buckthorn	*Frangula alnus*
Apple/Cultivated Apple	*Malus domestica*
Ash	*Fraxinus excelsior*
Aspen	*Populus tremula*
Austrian Pine/Corsican Pine	*Pinus nigra*
Beech	*Fagus sylvatica*
Black Currant	*Ribes nigrum*
Bramble/Blackberry	*Rubus fruticosus agg.*
Bridewort	*Spiraea aggregate*
Broom	*Cytisus scoparius*
Cherry Laurel	*Prunus laurocerasus*
Cherry Plum	*Prunus cerasifera*
Crab Apple	*Malus sylvestris*
Dog Rose	*Rosa canina agg.*
Downy Birch	*Betula pubescens*
Elder	*Sambucus nigra*
Goat Willow/Pussy Willow	*Salix caprea*
Gorse/Furze	*Ulex europaeus*
Grey Willow	*Salix cinerea subsp. cinerea*
Grey Willow	*Salix cinerea subsp. oleifolia*
Guelder-rose	*Viburnum opulus*
Holly	*Ilex aquifolium*
Horse-chestnut	*Aesculus hippocastanum*
Hawthorn	*Crataegus monogyna*
Hazel	*Corylus avellana*
Lilac	*Syringa vulgaris*
Norway Spruce	*Picea abies*
Osier/Common Osier	*Salix viminalis*
Pedunculate Oak/Common Oak	*Quercus robur*
Red Currant	*Ribes rubrum*
Rhododendron	*Rhododendron ponticum*
Rowan/Mountain Ash	*Sorbus aucuparia*
Scots Pine	*Pinus sylvestris*
Silver Birch	*Betula pendula*
Sycamore	*Acer pseudoplatanus*
Wild Plum	*Prunus domestica*
Yew	*Taxus baccata*

Horsetails, ferns and herbs

(over 180 species recorded to date)

Agrimony	*Agrimonia eupatoria*
American Willowherb	*Epilobium ciliatum*
Annual Knawel/Knawel	*Scleranthus annuus*
Annual Meadow-grass	*Poa annua*
Autumnal Hawkbit	*Leontodon autumnalis*
Barren Strawberry	*Potentilla sterilis*
Basil Thyme	*Clinopodium acinos*
Beaked Hawk's-beard	*Crepis vesicaria*
Bell Heather	*Erica cinerea*
Betony	*Stachys officinalis*
Bird's foot/	
Common Birdsfoot	*Ornithopus perpusillus*
Bog Stitchwort	*Stellaria uliginosa*
Bracken/Brake	*Pteridium aquilinum*
Broad Buckler-fern/	
Common Buckler-fern	*Dryopteris dilatata*
Broad-leaved Dock	*Rumex obtusifolius*
Brown Bent	*Agrostis vinealis*
Buck's-horn Plantain	*Plantago coronopus*
Bugle	*Ajuga reptans*
Bugloss/Field Bugloss	*Anchusa arvensis*
Bulrush/Great Reedmace/	
False Bulrush	*Typha latifolia*
Canadian Fleabane	*Conyza canadensis*
Carnation Sedge	*Carex panicea*
Cat's-ear/Common Catsear	*Hypochaeris radicata*
Changing Forget-me-not	*Myosotis discolor*
Cleavers/Goosegrass	*Galium aparine*
Clustered Dock	*Rumex conglomeratus*
Cock's-foot	*Dactylis glomerata*
Common Bent	*Agrostis capillaris*
Common Bird's-foot-trefoil	*Lotus corniculatus*
Common Centaury	*Centaurium erythraea*
Common Chickweed	*Stellaria media*
Common Couch	*Elytrigia repens*
Common Cudweed	*Filago vulgaris*
Common Dog-violet	*Viola riviniana*
Common Duckweed	*Lemna minor*
Common Hemp-nettle	*Galeopsis tetrahit agg.*
Common Ivy	*Hedera helix subsp. helix*
Common Knapweed/	
Black Knapweed/Hardhead	*Centaurea nigra*
Common Male Fern	*Dryopteris filix-mas*
Common Mouse-ear	*Cerastium fontanum*
Common Nettle/Stinging Nettle	*Urtica dioica*
Common Ragwort	*Senecio jacobaea*
Common Reed	*Phragmites australis*
Common Sorrel	*Rumex acetosa*
Common Stork's-bill	*Erodium cicutarium agg.*
Common Valerian	*Valeriana officinalis*
Compact Rush	*Juncus conglomeratus*
Corn Mint	*Mentha arvensis*
Creeping Buttercup	*Ranunculus repens*
Creeping Cinquefoil	*Potentilla reptans*
Creeping Soft-grass	*Holcus mollis*
Creeping Thistle	*Cirsium arvense*
Cross-leaved Heath	*Erica tetralix*
Cuckooflower/ Lady's Smock/	
Milk-maids	*Cardamine pratensis*
Curled Dock	*Rumex crispus*
Daisy	*Bellis perennis*
Dandelion	*Taraxacum aggregate*
Devil's-bit Scabious	*Succisa pratensis*
Dove's-foot Crane's-bill	*Geranium molle*

Common Name	Scientific Name
Early Hair-grass/Small Hair-grass	Aira praecox
Equal-leaved Knotgrass	Polygonum arenastrum
False Oat-grass	Arrhenatherum elatius
False-brome/Wood False-brome	Brachypodium sylvaticum
Fat-hen	Chenopodium album
Field Forget-me-not/	
Common Forget-me-not	Myosotis arvensis
Field Horsetail/	
Common Horsetail	Equisetum arvense
Field Mouse-ear	Cerastium arvense
Field Pansy	Viola arvensis
Field Wood-rush	Luzula campestris
Foxglove	Digitalis purpurea
Garden Yellow Archangel	Lamiastrum galeobdolon
	subsp argentatum
Garlic Mustard	Alliaria petiolata
Germander Speedwell/	
Birdseye Speedwell	Veronica chamaedrys
Glaucous Sedge	Carex flacca
Goat's-beard	Tragopogon pratensis subsp. minor
Goldenrod	Solidago virgaurea
Great Mullein/Common Mullein	Verbascum thapsus
Great Willowherb	Epilobium hirsutum
Greater Plantain/Ratstail Plantain	Plantago major
Greater Stitchwort	Stellaria holostea
Green-ribbed Sedge/Moor Sedge	Carex binervis
Ground-elder/Goutweed/	
Bishopweed	Aegopodium podagraria
Ground-ivy	Glechoma hederacea
Groundsel	Senecio vulgaris
Hairy Sedge	Carex hirta
Hairy Tare	Vicia hirsuta
Hard fern	Blechnum spicant
Hard Rush	Juncus inflexus
Harebell	Campanula rotundifolia
Hawkweed	Hieracium aggregate
Heath Bedstraw	Galium saxatile
Heath Groundsel	Senecio sylvaticus
Heath Milkwort	Polygala serpyllifolia
Heath Rush	Juncus squarrosus
Heath speedwell/	
Common Speedwell	Veronica officinalis
Heath Wood-rush	Luzula multiflora subsp. congesta
Heather/Ling/Common Heather	Calluna vulgaris
Heath-grass	Danthonia decumbens
Hedge Woundwort	Stachys sylvatica
Hemlock	Conium maculatum
Herb Bennet/Wood Avens	Geum urbanum
Herb-Robert	Geranium robertianum
Hoary Willow-herb/	
Small-flowered Willow-herb	Epilobium parviflorum
Hogweed/Cow Parsnip/Keck	Heracleum sphondylium
Honeysuckle	Lonicera periclymenum
Jointed Rush	Juncus articulatus
Knot-grass	Polygonum aviculare
Lady's Bedstraw	Galium verum
Large Bird's-foot-trefoil	Lotus pedunculatus
Lemon-scented Fern	Oreopteris limbosperma
Lesser Stitchwort	Stellaria graminea
Lesser Trefoil/Lesser Yellow Trefoil	Trifolium dubium
Lily of the Valley	Convallaria majalis
Long-headed Poppy	Papaver dubium subsp. dubium
Many-seeded Goosefoot	Chenopodium polyspermum
Marsh Gentian	Gentiana pneumonanthe
Marsh Thistle	Cirsium palustre
Mat-grass	Nardus stricta
Meadow Buttercup	Ranunculus acris
Meadow Vetchling	Lathyrus pratensis
Mouse-ear-hawkweed	Pilosella officinarum
Nipplewort	Lapsana communis
Oval Sedge	Carex ovalis
Oxeye Daisy	Leucanthemum vulgare
Perennial Rye-grass/	
Common Rye-grass	Lolium perenne
Perforate St John's Wort/	
Common St John's Wort	Hypericum perforatum
Petty Spurge	Euphorbia peplus
Pill Sedge	Carex pilulifera
Pineapple Weed	Matricaria discoidea
Prickly Sow-thistle	Sonchus asper
Purple Moor-grass	Molinia caerulea
Red Clover	Trifolium pratense
Red Fescue	Festuca rubra agg.
Redshank/Redleg/Persicaria	Persicaria maculosa
Remote Sedge	Carex remota
Ribwort Plantain	Plantago lanceolata
Rosebay Willowherb/Fireweed	Chamerion angustifolium
Sand Spurrey	Spergularia rubra
Scarlet Pimpernel	Anagallis arvensis
Selfheal	Prunella vulgaris
Sharp-flowered Rush	Juncus acutiflorus
Sheep's fescue agg.	Festuca ovina agg.
Sheep's Sorrel	Rumex acetosella
Shepherd's-purse	Capsella bursa-pastoris
Silverweed	Potentilla anserina
Slender St John's Wort/	
Elegant St John's Wort	Hypericum pulchrum
Small Cudweed	Filago minima
Small-flowered Crane's-bill	Geranium pusillum
Smooth Cat's-ear	Hypochaeris glabra
Smooth Hawk's-beard	Crepis capillaris
Smooth Meadow-grass	Poa pratensis
Smooth Sow-thistle/	
Common Sow-thistle	Sonchus oleraceus
Smooth Tare	Vicia tetrasperma
Snowberry	Symphoricarpos albus
Soft Rush	Juncus effusus
Spear Thistle	Cirsium vulgare
Square-stalked St John's Wort/	
Square St John's Wort	Hypericum tetrapterum
Squirrel-tail Fescue	Vulpia bromoides
Sweet Vernal Grass	Anthoxanthum odoratum
Three-nerved Sandwort	Moehringia trinervia
Thyme-leaved Sandwort	Arenaria serpyllifolia sens. lat.
Thyme-leaved Speedwell	Veronica serpyllifolia
Tor-grass	Brachypodium pinnatum
Tormentil	Potentilla erecta
Tufted Forget-me-not	Myosotis laxa
Tufted hair-grass	Deschampsia cespitosa
Tufted Vetch	Vicia cracca
Upright Hedge-parsley/	
Hedge Parsley	Torilis japonica
Velvet Bent	Agrostis canina
Water Mint	Mentha aquatica
Water Starwort	Callitriche aggregate
Water-plantain/	
Common Water-plantain	Alisma plantago-aquatica
Wavy Hair-grass	Deschampsia flexuosa
Welted Thistle	Carduus crispus
White Campion	Silene latifolia
White Clover	Trifolium repens
White Dead-nettle	Lamium album
Wild Angelica	Angelica sylvestris
Wild Privet	Ligustrum vulgare
Wood Dock	Rumex sanguineus
Wood Sage	Teucrium scorodonia
Yarrow	Achillea millefolium
Yorkshire Fog	Holcus lanatus

Marsh Gentian

Courtesy of R Labbett

Smooth Cat's-ear

Courtesy of R Labbett

Goldenrod

Courtesy of R Labbett

The plants recorded that were of particular interest because of their scarcity were:

Marsh Gentian *(Gentiana pneumonanthe)* which is a nationally scarce species in decline. In Lincolnshire, this beautiful and striking plant is now only found at two other sites.

Smooth Cat's-ear *(Hypochaeris glabra)* which is another nationally scarce species that is easily overlooked because of its small size and its habit of closing its flowers by early afternoon. In Lincolnshire, it is mostly confined to the cover sands in the north west of the county.

Goldenrod *(Solidago virgaurea)* is never common in the past in Lincolnshire and now very scarce in the county. The population on The Hotchkin course is by far the largest in Lincolnshire.

Fauna

The wildlife seen around the course are also typical of species found on lowland heathland. Since 1996, lists of mammals, reptiles and birds have been kept and are given below:

Mammals

Badger	*Meles meles*
Bank Vole	*Clethrionomys glareolus*
Brown Hare	*Lepus capensis*
Reeves Muntjak Deer	*Muntiacus reevesi*
Common Pipistrelle Bat	*Pipistrellus pipistrellus*
Common Shrew	*Sorex ananeus*
Fallow Deer	*Dama dama dama*
Field Vole	*Microtus agrestis*
Grey Squirrel	*Sciurus carolinensis*
Mole	*Talpa europaea*
Rabbit	*Oryctolagus cuniculus*
Red Fox	*Vulpes vulpes*
Roe Deer	*Capreolus capreolus*
Stoat	*Mustela ermina*
Weasel	*Mustela nivalis*
Western Hedgehog	*Erinaceus europaeus*
Wood Mouse	*Apodemus sylvaticus*

Reptiles

Slow worm	*Anguis fragilis*
Grass snake	*Natrix natrix*
Common frog	*Rana temporaria*
Common Lizard	*Lacerta vivipara*
Adder	*Vipera berus*

A study of moths and insects has also been carried out since 2003 and at the time 220 species of moth have been recorded, some of which are extremely rare. An Emperor Moth was possibly the highlight of the recording sessions to date. Fourteen species of butterfly have also been recorded, the most notable being the Brown Argus. Four different dragonflies have also been noted.

Courtesy of R Labbett

Emperor Moth

Woodlark 2817075-00068-570 David Tipling and rspb-images.com

Woodlark

Birds

(80 species of birds have been recorded to date)

Barn Owl	*Tyto alba*
Blackbird	*Turdus merula*
Blackcap	*Sylvia atricapilla*
Blackheaded Gull	*Larus ridibundus*
Blue Tit	*Parus caeruleus*
Bullfinch	*Pyrrhula pyrrhula*
Carrion Crow	*Corvus corone corone*
Chaffinch	*Fringilla coelebs*
Chiffchaff	*Phylloscopus collybita*
Coal Tit	*Parus ater*
Collared Dove	*Streptopelia decaocto*
Common Buzzard	*Buteo buteo*
Coot	*Fulica atra*
Cormorant	*Phalacrocorax carbo*
Crossbill	*Loxia curvirostra*
Cuckoo	*Cuculus canorus*
Fieldfare	*Turdus pilaris*
Garden Warbler	*Sylvia borin*
Goldcrest	*Regulus regulus*
Goldfinch	*Carduelis carduelis*
Great Crested Grebe	*Podiceps cristatus*
Great Spotted Woodpecker	*Dendrocopos major*
Great Tit	*Parus major*
Green Woodpecker	*Picus viridis*
Greenfinch	*Carduelis chloris*
Grey Heron	*Ardea cinerea*
Grey Partridge	*Perdix perdix*
Greylag Goose	*Anser anser*
Hedge Sparrow	*Prunella modularis*
Hen Harrier	*Circus cyaneus*
Hobby	*Falco subbuteo*
House Martin	*Delichon urbica*
House Sparrow	*Passer domesticus*
Jay	*Garrulus glandarius*
Jackdaw	*Corvus monedula*
Kestrel	*Falco tinnunculus*
Kingfisher	*Alcedo atthis*
Linnet	*Acanthis cannabina*
Little Grebe	*Tachybaptus ruficollis*
Little Owl	*Athene noctua*
Long Tailed Tit	*Aegithalos caudatus*
Magpie	*Pica pica*
Mallard	*Anas platyrhynchos*
Marsh Tit	*Parus palustris*

Meadow Pipit	*Anthus pratensis*
Mistle Thrush	*Turdus viscivorus*
Moorhen	*Gallinula chloropus*
Mute Swan	*Cygnus olor*
Nuthatch	*Sitta europaea*
Peregrine	*Falco peregrinus*
Pheasant	*Phasianus colchilus*
Pied Wagtail	*Motacilla alba*
Oystercatcher	*Haematopus ostralegus*
Red Kite	*Milvus milvus*
Red Legged Partridge	*Alectoris rufa*
Redwing	*Turdus iliacus*
Robin	*Erithacus rubecula*
Rook	*Corvus frugilegus*
Skylark	*Alauda arvensis*
Snipe	*Gallinago gallinago*
Song Thrush	*Turdus philomelos*
Sparrowhawk	*Accipiter nisus*
Spotted Flycatcher	*Muscicapa striata*
Starling	*Sturnus vulgaris*
Stock Dove	*Columba oenas*
Swallow	*Hirundo rustica*
Swift	*Apus apus*
Tawny Owl	*Strix aluco*
Treecreeper	*Certhia familiaris*
Tree Sparrow	*Passer montanus*
Tufted Duck	*Aythya fuligula*
Turtle Dove	*Streptopelia turtur*
Water Rail	*Rallus aquaticus*
Wheatear	*Oenanthe oenanthe*
Whitethroat	*Sylvia communis*
Wigeon	*Anas penelope*
Willow Warbler	*Phylloscopus trochilus*
Wood Duck	*Aix sponsa*
Woodcock	*Scolopax rusticola*
Woodlark	*Lullula arborea*
Wood Pigeon	*Columba palumbus*
Wren	*Troglodytes troglodytes*
Yellowhammer	*Emberiza citrinella*

The above lists are not exhaustive but provide an indication of the varied flora and fauna species. The management team is particularly aware of the importance of maintaining the varied flora species and wildlife habitats. Different management policies have been developed for each category and are continually monitored and enhanced, working with organisations such as English Nature.

Crossbill

Crossbill 2817075-00068-570 David Tipling and rspb-images.com

Harry Vardon

T P Stokoe

Harry Shapland Colt

Stafford Vere Hotchkin

Neil Stafford Hotchkin

"Without the influence, dedication and support of this select group of people, the game of golf may not have been blessed with such a wonderful course."